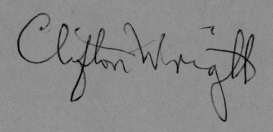

HURRICANE!

HUR

RICANE!

by Joe McCarthy

American Heritage Press
New York

Library of Congress Catalog Card Number: 79-83810
SBN: 8281-0020-9

HURRICANE!

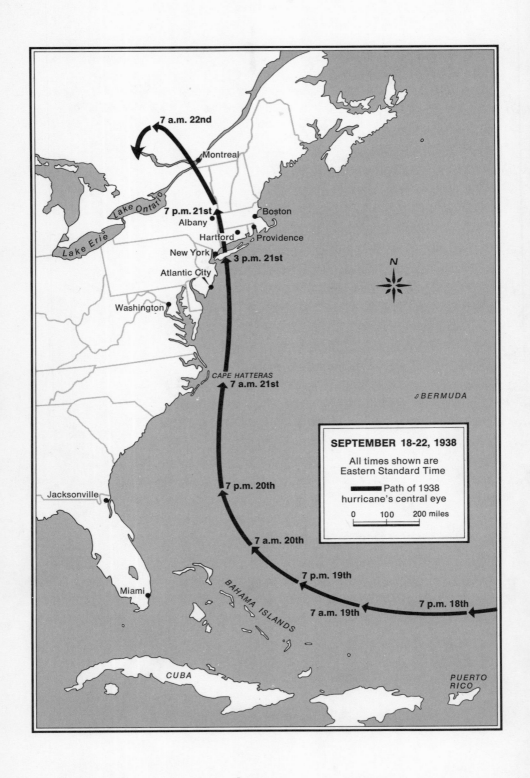

7 a.m. 22nd

Montreal

Lake Ontario

7 p.m. 21st
Albany

Boston

Lake Erie

Hartford   Providence

New York

3 p.m. 21st

Atlantic City

Washington

CAPE HATTERAS
7 a.m. 21st

N

BERMUDA

7 p.m. 20th

SEPTEMBER 18-22, 1938

All times shown are
Eastern Standard Time

━━━━ Path of 1938
hurricane's central eye

0   100   200 miles

7 a.m. 20th

Jacksonville

7 p.m. 19th

Miami

BAHAMA ISLANDS

7 a.m. 19th   7 p.m. 18th

CUBA

*PUERTO
RICO*

1

THE GREAT TROPICAL hurricane that on Wednesday, September 21, 1938, wrecked J. P. Morgan's estate at Glen Cove, Long Island, and the trestle of the scenic railway on Mount Washington in New Hampshire, drowned several people near City Hall in downtown Providence, Rhode Island, overturned a tugboat in Boston Harbor, tore up the boardwalk at Atlantic City and, rather significantly, ripped to shreds the flag on the Whitehall Building, where the Weather Bureau's New York City office was then located, was first sighted five days earlier, at 9:30 P.M. on September 16, by a Brazilian merchant ship, the S.S. *Alegrete*, in the lower North Atlantic Ocean 350 miles northeast of Puerto Rico. The hurricane was fully developed at that time and had all the marks of a dangerous cyclonic storm. Its mature size and intensity, and its position and course as it traveled westward with the trade winds at the unusually fast forward speed of twenty miles per hour, indicated to meteorologists at the Jacksonville, Florida, station of the Weather Bureau that the disturbance was

3

a hurricane that had probably formed somewhere west of the Cape Verde Islands, near the bulge of the northwest African coast, perhaps in an atmospheric depression that had passed onto the ocean from the Sahara Desert on September 4.

In brief, a tropical hurricane forms around a low-pressure center, which draws up warm, moist air from the ocean. The storm becomes a cyclone as cooler winds, blowing in a circular whirlwind pattern, rush into the chimneylike low-pressure center to replace the rising warm air. Like water swirling down a bathtub drain, the rotating winds blow counterclockwise in the Northern Hemisphere and clockwise south of the equator because of the earth's spin. As the process builds up, the storm takes on the shape of a dark and cloudy doughnut with a calm and quite clear hole in the center; it becomes classified as a hurricane when the rotating gales gain a sustained force of seventy-five miles or more per hour.

A full-fledged hurricane, like the one sighted by the *Alegrete*, has a doughnut of hurricane-speed gales spreading out more than 100 miles from the center, and is usually surrounded by an outer circle—another 350 or 400 miles in width—of attending gale winds, 40 miles per hour or faster. A whole hurricane disturbance may therefore be as wide as one thousand miles. People often confuse hurricanes with tornadoes, and wonder about the difference between hurricanes and typhoons. A tornado is another type of cyclonic storm, the most vicious produced by nature, with whirlwinds as high as 450 to 500 miles per hour traveling at a forward speed of 30 to 40 miles per hour. But a tornado, which is born on land and quickly dies there, is only about 400 yards wide and travels about 16 miles or less before it dissolves. A hurricane can travel for weeks over the ocean, across land, and back to the ocean again if it can find enough

4

warm moisture to keep on replenishing its strength. "Typhoon" is merely the term for hurricanes occurring in the Pacific Ocean. The name "hurricane," incidentally, comes from Huracan, the name of a Caribbean Indian storm god.

The approach of a Cape Verde hurricane, such as the one reported by the *Alegrete*, is always bad news to weather observers in Florida and the Caribbean islands. The longer a hurricane travels over water before reaching land, the bigger and stronger and more dangerous it becomes. A Cape Verde hurricane moving toward Florida after traveling about two thousand miles from the African side of the Atlantic is naturally to be feared more than a hurricane that has bloomed around the Lesser Antilles or in the Caribbean between Cuba and Central or South America.

This particular Cape Verde hurricane in 1938 gave the Weather Bureau men at Jacksonville the jitters not only because it was a big one traveling at the unusually fast speed of twenty miles per hour—hurricanes far out at sea usually dawdle along at twelve miles per hour and rarely exceed fifteen—but because it was headed straight for Miami. By 8 P.M. on the evening of Sunday, September 18, the storm was 900 miles east-southeast of that city. The following morning the hurricane was another 250 miles closer and still aiming directly at the Miami area. That afternoon the Jacksonville office of the Weather Bureau issued an urgent warning that the hurricane would reach the southeast Florida coast within the next twenty-four to thirty hours if it maintained its direction and rate of speed, and advised everybody in southern Florida to prepare for the storm.

The hurricane-conscious Floridians boarded up windows, tied down boats, made sure that their battery-powered radios would be working when the electric power went out, and sat

5

down to wait. That night the Jacksonville forecasters continued to urge vigilance, but they noted hopefully that the hurricane was turning northward about 420 miles east of Miami and said that the threat to the Florida coast had "greatly diminished."

The advisory report issued by the Weather Bureau the next morning, Tuesday, September 20, at 9:30 A.M., had good news, at least for Florida. It said that the hurricane had slowed down slightly, from twenty to seventeen miles per hour, and was definitely moving to the north in the coastal waters about three hundred miles offshore. The bureau predicted that the hurricane would turn to the northeast off Cape Hatteras that night. In other words, the storm was heading out to sea and there was nothing more to worry about.

Actually, the big hurricane was thriving and was getting bigger and stronger as it moved up the Carolina coast that Tuesday evening. It had turned away from the Florida and Georgia shore line because a high-pressure mass of dry, cool air from the Midwest and the Alleghenies had drifted down into the Southern states. Such high pressure repels a hurricane, which seeks the low pressure and warm humidity that it needs to replenish its energy and strength. A closer study of the Atlantic weather map that day might have shown the Weather Bureau forecasters that the hurricane was hardly likely to head out to sea either. Another vast high-pressure area, bigger than the one over the Midwest and the Alleghenies, was drifting down the North Atlantic from Newfoundland and Nova Scotia toward the anticyclonic high-pressure air that prevails between Bermuda and the Azores.

But between these two high-pressure plateaus, straight ahead to the north above Cape Hatteras, there was a wide, inviting path of low pressure, filled with the warmth and wetness that a hurricane thrives on. This valley between the atmospheric heights extended like a red carpet from Cape Hatteras, across the ocean off the Delaware and New Jersey coasts, up to Long Island, and over New England, where it had been warm and humid and had rained heavily off and on for several days. Sniffing the attractive sticky dampness, the hurricane suddenly picked up speed and hurried toward it.

On the way, near Cape Hatteras, the wildly accelerating storm brushed against the startled Cunard White Star liner *Carinthia*, southward bound with six hundred passengers on a cruise from New York to the Caribbean. The *Carinthia*'s captain, who said later that the hurricane was the worst storm he had seen in all his years at sea, had accepted the Weather Bureau's prediction that it would be turning northeastward and had changed his course to move closer to Cape Hatteras, figuring that he would pass safely to the west of the turning hurricane. But at twelve thirty on the morning of Wednesday, the fateful September 21, he found himself buffeted by it. Obviously this hurricane was not yet showing any sign of drifting harmlessly away from the coast and out into the sea and oblivion, as the Weather Bureau had calmly assumed it would because most northbound tropical storms follow that course when they get to Cape Hatteras.

As the *Carinthia*'s captain noted, it was no ordinary tropical hurricane. His ship's barometer measured its pressure at 27.85, one of the lowest barometric readings ever recorded on the Atlantic coast and a danger sign indicating that the hurricane was overloaded with explosive power. Those who have little knowledge of meteorology are astounded to learn that an average hurricane releases in one day as much energy as the entire United States uses in electric power over a period of six months. The hurricane of 1938, as it moved past Cape Hatteras on the

7

morning of September 21 toward the long trough of warm humidity stretching into New England, carried much more force than an average hurricane; gusts in its wide circle of rotating 100-mile-per-hour gales were clocked later in the day as high as 186 miles per hour, and that was over the New England mainland, when the huge whirlwind was losing its fuel supply. In the morning, when the storm was plunging into the inviting corridor of ocean-fed low-pressure moisture, its roaring gales must have been much stronger; it was then, while it reveled in an atmosphere more compatible than most hurricanes are ever able to find, that the whole body of the widespread storm leaped forward like a runaway horse and roared directly north toward the shores of Long Island and New England, accelerating suddenly to a speed that might have been expected in a tornado but never in a hurricane—almost 60 miles per hour.

If the hurricane had been able to plan consciously a surprise attack on a thickly populated area of the northeast coast, it could not have picked a better day and better circumstances. Along with the unusually wet and warm weather, it was the time of the equinox, when both the moon and the sun exert the greatest pull on the tides. Even without the surge of towering storm waves, thirty to forty feet high, pushed in from the ocean by the hurricane's gales, the tides on the shore that afternoon would have been much higher than usual. Previous days of heavy rain had left all New England so soaked and so thoroughly filled with muggy humidity that the hurricane would be able to keep on replenishing its strength after it passed over the coast and swept northward.

Apart from the weather that preceded it, the biggest factors in favor of the hurricane's surprise attack were, of course, the Weather Bureau's dogged assumption that the storm would turn away from the coast at Cape Hatteras and the inadequacy of facilities for gathering information that might have showed the bureau that its assumption was wrong. In 1938 the Weather Bureau depended entirely on voluntary reports from merchant ships and commercial planes for news of ocean weather and the position of ocean storms. There were no government weather-reporting ships then, and no government hurricane-tracking aircraft. Commercial airliners in the East had been grounded that week because of the bad weather. As Dr. James H. Kimball, then the chief of the Weather Bureau's office in New York, explained later in an interview, there had been only two reports on the hurricane after it was sighted by the *Carinthia*. Both reports were from ships in the Cape Hatteras area on September 21, one at 2 A.M. and the other at 9. The 9 A.M. report located the storm farther north and farther from the coast than the earlier report, strengthening the bureau's assumption that the hurricane would be turning out to sea.

For the next six hours—from 9 A.M. Eastern Standard Time until shortly before 3 P.M., when the center of the hurricane was reaching the beaches on Long Island—the Weather Bureau received, according to Dr. Kimball, "not a scrap of information" about the storm's whereabouts. Apparently there were no ships in the coastal waters between Virginia and Long Island that day, perhaps because of the hurricane warnings for that area issued the day before in Jacksonville. The Weather Bureau's main office in Washington, which had taken over responsibility for the hurricane after it passed out of Jacksonville's jurisdiction at Cape Hatteras, could only guess at where the storm might be after it made its sudden, sixty-mile-per-hour disappearance from the Carolina coast. In the absence of any information to the contrary, the bureau decided to stick to its forecast of the previous

9

night, which never mentioned the possibility that the hurricane would hit the New York or New England coasts.

Thus on Wednesday, September 21, while the hurricane was racing toward New York, Connecticut, Rhode Island, and Massachusetts, the weather prediction in that morning's newspapers said only: "Rain, probably heavy, today and tomorrow; cooler." The coastal weather forecast that day for the shore between New York Harbor and Eastport, Maine, was "fresh southerly winds, except fresh north or northeast near Sandy Hook, increasing this afternoon or tonight and overcast with rain." Ironically *The New York Times* on the morning of the big hurricane published an editorial complimenting the Weather Bureau for its alertness in warning Florida of the hurricane earlier in the week. In its news columns, the *Times* carried a report quoting the Jacksonville Weather Bureau station as having said that the hurricane was "turning on a northward arc" and "apparently" heading safely out to sea. The report on the hurricane from Florida was then regarded as so unimportant that the *Times* buried it in the lower left corner of page 27.

At one o'clock* on the afternoon of the day of the hurricane, Long Island radio stations broadcast warnings from the Weather Bureau of "whole gales," which are winds of less than hurricane strength. An hour later, in an advisory report issued when the hurricane's gusts were already lashing the Long Island, Connecticut, and Rhode Island shores, the Weather Bureau said that the "tropical storm" would be "likely to pass over Long Island and Connecticut late [that] afternoon or early [that] night, at-

---

* Unless otherwise noted, all times used hereafter are Eastern Daylight Time, which was in effect in New York and New England at the time of the hurricane.

tended by shifting gales." But this last word before the catastrophe did not in any way suggest that the "tropical storm" might be a hurricane.

Directly in the path of the unsuspected hurricane were thirteen million people on Long Island and in New England. There were another six million in New Jersey and New York on the west side of the storm, just outside the full force of its destruction but close enough to be lashed by gusts of its hurricane gales and flooded by its overwhelming high tides and torrential rain. On the course that the hurricane was following along the low-pressure corridor from Cape Hatteras, its center, or eye, would pass across the middle of Long Island and Long Island Sound, moving over the shore of Connecticut between Bridgeport and New Haven. From there the center of the storm —the hole in the doughnut of rotating hurricane gales—would go northward through the Naugatuck River valley near the manufacturing cities of Waterbury and Torrington and a few miles west of Hartford, across the Berkshire Hills of Massachusetts near Springfield, and up into the Green Mountains in the center of Vermont before trailing off across Lake Champlain into Canada. Hartford and Springfield were in deep trouble from the elements even before the hurricane arrived: the drenching rains of previous days, on top of the wetness of an unusually dark and rainy summer, had raised the Connecticut River to a dangerous flood level. On Wednesday morning, a few hours before the hurricane came, a man in Hartford telephoned his mother at her summer cottage in Watch Hill, on the ocean shore of Rhode Island, and urged her to remain there instead of returning that day to her winter home in Hartford as she had planned. He warned her that the Connecticut River was almost as high as it had been during Hartford's big flood of 1936. She took his advice and stayed at the seashore, where the hurricane damage was to be worse than it was in Hartford.

Contrary to what most people assume, a city like Hartford, close to the center of the hurricane, is not the worst place to be in a widespread tropical cyclonic storm such as this one, although being in the storm center is bad enough. Because of centrifugal force, the rotating gales circling counterclockwise around the doughnut-shaped pattern gain their greatest acceleration in speed and power as they curve along the east side of the circle. Thus those hurricane gales fifty to seventy-five miles east of the center are much more ferocious and destructive than the gales in the center or those on the west side of the center, where the winds are only beginning to make the accelerating swing around the circle.

Consequently, on the Wednesday when the hurricane was approaching the coast, with its circle of heavy gales spreading to a diameter of 150 miles, the areas ahead of the east side of the storm—eastern Long Island, such eastern Connecticut cities as New London and Norwich, all of Rhode Island, and the Buzzards Bay shores of Massachusetts—were in greater danger of destruction than New Haven or Hartford. Similarly, farther inland, Worcester, Massachusetts, was more threatened than Springfield, and towns in southwest New Hampshire, like Peterboro and Keene, were in more potential danger than places in Vermont along the eye's path. On the west side of the hurricane's center, in Long Island's Nassau County and along the border between New York State and New England, there would be less chance of serious damage.

The possibility that such a hurricane could travel such a route never occurred to people in New York and New England that morning because, apart from the lack of warnings from the Weather Bureau, the thought of a tropical hurricane turning up that far north on the coast seemed in 1938 to be ridiculous. Most people assumed that there had never been a hurricane on Long Island or in New England. (Several newspapers, describing the storm the day after it struck, called it the first hurricane in the history of New England.) Actually, as history shows, New England and Long Island had no immunity from hurricanes. Governor William Bradford had described one that hit the Plymouth settlement in Massachusetts in August, 1635, with storm waves that "caused the sea to swell above 20 foote, right up and downe, and made many of the Indeans to clime into trees for their saftie."

But hurricanes were unknown on the northeast coast in 1938 because the last big one, on September 23, 1815, had been long forgotten, and several subsequent generations of New Englanders had never seen such a storm. If there had been a historically oriented amateur meteorologist in Boston or New York who suspected from a study of the low-pressure and high-pressure areas on the weather map in *The New York Times* on the morning of September 21, 1938, that the tropical hurricane from Florida might be likely to travel to New England, a reading of old reports on the 1815 storm would have given him a preview of what such a cyclonic blow might do. The 1938 hurricane was to follow a path to the north close to that of the hurricane of 1815; the storms seem to have been similar in their extreme intensity. The storm in 1815 had wrecked the seaside towns of eastern Long Island and the ports of New London and Stonington on the east shore of Connecticut, which are outside the protection of Long Island Sound. Then the hurricane had driven high water up into the narrow head of Narragansett Bay, flooding the center of Providence and carrying four ships, nine brigs, seven schooners, and fifteen sloops from the docks and the bay into the downtown section of the city. Moses Brown, the famous Rhode Island merchant and shipping king, was said to have lost one million dollars in the 1815 hurricane, which went on to damage Boston and to continue its travels in New Hampshire and Vermont. Under the same weather conditions—the historically oriented meteorologist might have asked himself—couldn't it happen again?

But on that Wednesday, September 21, in 1938, few people in New York or New England were wondering what had happened to the hurricane that had threatened Florida two days earlier. Those who listened to radio news broadcasts paid more attention to the reports from Europe than to the weather forecasts. Hitler was threatening war if Czechoslovakia refused to give him its Sudetenland, and Britain and France were trying to pacify the German dictator by granting his demands. Otherwise, it was an ordinary day for a September Wednesday in one of those late Depression, prewar years. The then almost new *Queen Mary* was sailing from New York to Europe that night with 968 passengers. The best seats in the theaters on Broadway, where a new Cole Porter musical—*You'll Never Know*, with Clifton Webb, Libby Holman, and Lupe Velez—was opening, were selling at the top price of $3.00. In that morning's New York newspapers, which then sold for $0.03, Gimbel's was advertising a sale of men's Harris tweed topcoats for $25.00 and men's broadcloth shirts for $1.35. Students from all over the nation were traveling to New England for the reopening of colleges and schools; among them was a group of thirty excited small boys from wealthy families in the New York area, who were assembling at Grand Central Terminal under the guidance of a harassed teacher named Roderick Hagenbuckle. They were to board the Shore Line express, the Bostonian, which would take them to the Fessenden School in West Newton, Massachusetts, by way of New London, Providence, and Boston.

If the approaching hurricane was deliberately planning to terrorize as many people as possible, there was one flaw in its selection of the day: because so many schools were already open or opening soon, most of the summer cottages at the more exposed beaches were closed and empty. Wednesday, in the middle of the week, was also a day when the oceanside resorts, where the danger from the hurricane was greatest, were not heavily populated that late in the season. But there were still a considerable number of late-stayers trying to stretch out the vacation season at their shorefront cottages—older people with grown children and families with children too young for school. Many of them liked to remain at the ocean late in September, a season of rough northeast storms, because the high and wild surf of such storms was a fascinating spectacle to watch.

There was a large colony of late-staying summer residents at Westhampton Beach, on the long and narrow strand of barrier beach that stretches for sixty miles along the south shore of Long Island between Fire Island Inlet and Southampton—the place on the coast where the hurricane was to strike first. This low-lying strip of sand dunes faces the ocean surf; separating it from the Long Island mainland is a series of bays: Great South Bay, Moriches Bay, Quantuck Bay, and Shinnecock Bay. In 1938, before the hurricane, the barrier beach had only one inlet, or gap of water, along its entire length—Moriches Inlet, between the ocean and Moriches Bay. Moriches Inlet had been opened by a northeast storm in 1931, and because local boatmen welcomed it as an access to the ocean from the bay, they had kept it open by building reinforcing jetties. The long stretch of beach west of Moriches Inlet, known to old-timers on Long Island as Great South Beach and now incorrectly called Fire Island by newcomers (that is really the name of a small island near Fire Island Inlet), had only a few small and scattered summer settlements thirty years ago, most of them at its far west end: Kismet, Saltaire, Point O'Woods, Ocean Beach, and Cherry Grove.

But east of Moriches Inlet, along Dune Road—the single paved road that ran along the beach from Moriches Bay to Southampton—the stretch of barrier dunes was closely crowded with large beach houses and had a sizable population in the summer months. Unlike the more isolated Fire Island section of the beach to the west, which then could be reached only by ferryboats, Dune Road was connected by bridges to the nearby mainland villages of Westhampton, Quogue, and Hampton Bays. Because it was a more accessible part of the ocean beach and was supplied with electricity and telephones, it attracted, then as now, more housebuilders and more of the wealthy summer rental tenants who bring servants with them. Westhampton Beach, between Moriches Bay and Quogue, was the most thickly built up section of Dune Road before the hurricane, with 179 houses, many of them large and sturdily built, along its ten miles of beach. The large number of late-season vacationers there in 1938 learned that such a narrow strip of low, oceanfront sand dunes with wide stretches of bay water behind it, separating it from the safety of the mainland, is a highly vulnerable place to be when a tropical cyclonic storm blows in suddenly from the ocean. No matter how well constructed a house on such a beach may be, a towering, hurricane-driven wave crashing over the top of the dunes may sweep it into the bay.

The weather on the morning of the day of the hurricane

was very much as it had been during most of that wet and humid summer on the northeast coast—cloudy and misty, with the sun breaking through the low clouds occasionally but briefly. The temperature was in the low 70's, and some people at the beaches tried to swim in the heavy surf before noon. A few experienced weather watchers noticed something unusual in the sky during the morning: when there was a break in the low-lying mist, they could see higher clouds moving rapidly from the south, a curious sight because the brisk wind was coming from a more easterly direction. The weather offshore at the east end of Long Island did not seem too threatening in the morning. Several fishing boats took off from Montauk seeking the striped bass that were said to be running plentifully off Block Island. But the Portuguese fishermen at Stonington, Connecticut, a few miles north of Montauk on the opposite side of Block Island Sound, decided against going to sea that day because they had not liked the copper-colored look of the previous evening's sunset.

About noon there was rain, and a strong wind from the east increased quickly to gale force, but the atmosphere remained warm and sticky, with the temperature staying above 70°. The rising east wind stirred up a thundering surf on the beaches, and people in oceanside houses who could see the angry waves from their picture windows cheerfully telephoned friends and invited them to come over for the afternoon to watch the storm. Nobody thought that the storm would be anything more than one of the usual September northeasters, and after the lunch hour it never occurred to anybody in the villages of eastern Long Island that it might be well to keep the children at home during the afternoon instead of letting them return to school.

Early in the afternoon, however, the barometer began to fall quickly. There is a story, which may or may not be apocryphal, that is told often on Long Island. It concerns a man at Westhampton Beach who received in the mail on that Wednesday a barometer that he had bought a few days earlier in a New York City store. After opening the package, he found the barometer's needle pointing down below 29, at the section of the dial marked "Tornadoes and Hurricanes." He shook the barometer impatiently and banged it with his fist, but the needle refused to move. The man rewrapped the instrument, enclosing a note complaining that it was obviously out of order, and took it to the post office in the village, where he mailed it back to the store. When he returned home from the post office, so the story goes, he found that his shorefront house had just been demolished by the hurricane of 1938.

2

AFTER PROWLING the Atlantic Ocean for several days and then making its sudden rush to the north from Cape Hatteras, the hurricane of 1938 first struck land on the south shore of Long Island with such force that shocks from the impact of the waves smashing on the beaches were registered on a seismograph at Sitka, Alaska, and salt spray from the surf was carried by the gales more than one hundred miles inland, whitening windows in Vermont.

The first round of gales, rotating counterclockwise and blowing from the east around the northern or advance side of the approaching doughnut-shaped storm pattern, began to sweep across Long Island about three o'clock in the afternoon. These early gales, increasing their speed steadily during the next half hour to more than eighty miles per hour, first knocked down trees. Then chimneys began to be blown off the roofs of houses, and a few minutes later church steeples crashed to the ground,

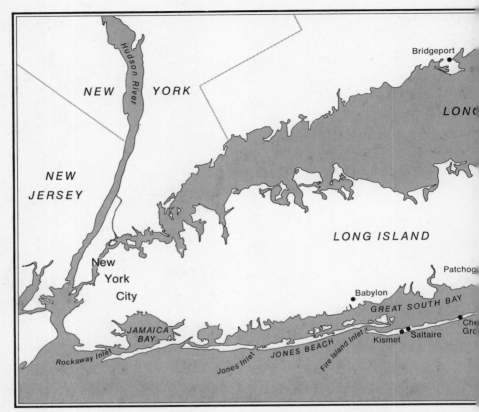

walls of buildings were torn away, and boats were ripped loose from moorings and smashed against docks. On the outer barrier beach at Fire Island and Westhampton, the ocean waves were roaring over the tops of the sand dunes, wrecking houses and carrying people into the bays.

About 3:40 P.M. the eye of the hurricane reached Long Island, passing over the center of Great South Bay to the south shore between Babylon and Patchogue, and bringing a deceptive lull in the storm. The eye of the cyclonic circle of gales, the hole in the center of the doughnut, is a calm spot in the middle of turbulence. Farther out on both sides of the center—on the

20

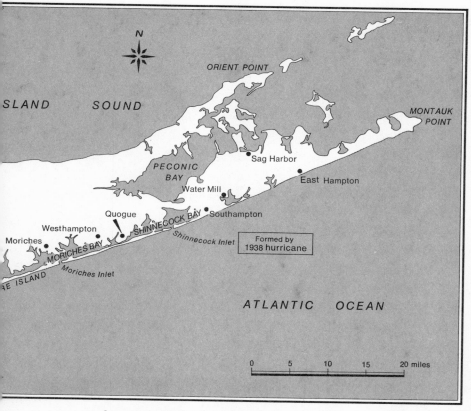

east at devastated Westhampton and on the less ferocious west side of the storm in Nassau County and in the Queens and Brooklyn suburbs—the lull was less noticeable. But close to the eye the winds died down temporarily and in a few places the sun emerged. Being unfamiliar with the behavior of hurricanes, many people in these areas assumed that the storm was over and came out of their houses to look at the damage. They did not realize that the worst part of the hurricane—the stronger and more accelerated winds behind the passing eye—was yet to come.

Along with the destruction left by the first round of early gales, a strange sight greeted those who went to waterfront docks in Great South Bay during the lull to check on their boats. The powerful hurricane gales had swept most of the water away from the shores of the bay and out of its creeks and estuaries, leaving boats lying on their sides on mud flats that had never been seen before. Toad Conklin, proprietor of a boat yard that had been built a century before near the bay on the Patchogue River, found himself staring in astonishment at wooden tracks, used for launching boats, that had been placed under water on the bottom of the river more than one hundred years earlier and were exposed for the first time since then.

After the hurricane's eye passed over the shore and moved off to the north toward Connecticut, the sky darkened again, rain fell, and the wind suddenly shifted from the east to the south. Then the full blast of the hurricane's second gales came in from the ocean at more than 90 miles per hour—with gusts probably blowing as high as 150 miles per hour—pushing ahead of them a high, surging wall of water, which onlookers mistakenly described later as a tidal wave. A tidal wave is caused by an underwater earthquake or some other type of underwater disturbance, but the towering ridge of water driven by a hurricane is pushed from the surface by the hurricane gales and rises higher as it accumulates, like snow pushed by a snowplow. Meteorologists call it a storm wave. There was disagreement later among surviving eyewitnesses on Long Island and on the New England shore as to whether this wall of high water, which rose to thirty and forty feet in many places, was one big wave or a series of several big waves. "It looked like a thick and high bank of fog rolling in fast from the ocean," one of the survivors said recently. "When it came closer we saw that it wasn't fog. It was water."

The towering surge of storm waves dealt the final knockout blow to the already badly battered Westhampton section of the outer barrier beach, and after washing over the beach and leveling houses and sand dunes, the high wall of water rolled on across the bays and flooded the mainland shore. In the center of Westhampton Beach village, which is located on the mainland almost a mile behind the bay, the water rose to seven feet on the main street; in several places farther east on Long Island— Quogue, Southampton, Water Mill—the bays flooded the inland Montauk Highway. The sea came over the high dunes at East Hampton, flooding the Maidstone Club golf courses, and swept across the Montauk Highway and the Long Island Railroad tracks at Napeague Beach, cutting off Montauk from the rest of Long Island. In the business center of Montauk, which lies low among surrounding hills, the waves from the ocean smashed the stores and the post office and tore the whole front wall off White's drug store. The people of Montauk fled to high ground; most of them spent the rest of the day and the following night in Montauk Manor, the spacious resort hotel that stands on a hill above the village. The Long Island shore west of Great South Bay, along Jones Beach, Long Beach, and the Rockaways, was spared such inundating hurricane waves because the gales rotating counterclockwise on that side of the center of the storm were blowing from the north, toward the ocean instead of from it, during the height of the turbulence.

The second round of the hurricane, after the passing of the eye, lasted on Long Island for another hour, from shortly before 4 P.M. until about 5. Then the gales began to subside and by 5:30 the hurricane was over, although the winds blew hard for another few hours. The passage of the hurricane had taken less than three hours. The damage that it left all over eastern Long Island was astonishing, but at Westhampton Beach, the hardest hit of the populated places on the shore, the destruction was incredible. Of the 179 houses on the ocean beach at West-hampton, 153 were swept away completely by the hurricane waves, and most of the structures that remained standing were too battered to be lived in again. Twenty-nine people died in the storm there; some of the bodies were carried miles away and were not found until several days later.

The barrier beach along Dune Road, which before the storm had had one inlet—the opening to Moriches Bay—was torn by ten wide break-throughs. One of the new openings between the ocean and Shinnecock Bay at Hampton Bays was three hundred feet wide. It was preserved and is now known as Shinnecock Inlet. Local people had tried unsuccessfully to dig such an inlet there early in the century to give boats an access to the ocean from Shinnecock Bay and Great Peconic Bay. Now the hurricane had done the job for them. All along Dune Road the dunes were so eroded and leveled that after the storm the surf on the ocean side of the barrier beach was clearly visible from the mainland across the bays.

Survivors agreed later that most of the destruction and the flattening of the dunes had been done by the big hurricane wave, or waves, that washed over the beach after the wind shifted to the south and renewed the fury of the storm. Stanley J. Teller, the chief of the two-man Westhampton Beach police force, was on the beach with his fellow officer, Timothy Robinson, trying to evacuate a group of people from an oceanfront house when the high surge of water came upon them. Teller remembers the deluge as one great wave rather than several waves.

"There were about seventeen people gathered in that house, and among them there were three small children named McCooey," Teller said recently. "I was carrying two of the

24

children, twin boys about six years old, from the house to my car, which was parked on Dune Road. I had a twin slung over each shoulder. The big wave came over the dunes behind me and picked me up and lifted me into the crossarms of a telephone pole. The telephone pole was thirty feet high, so the wave must have been thirty feet high, or higher. The two twins disappeared. While I was hanging to the top of the telephone pole, Tim Robinson's rubber boots came floating by me. I recognized them as Tim's because he had been wearing black boots with white soles. So there were Tim's boots but there was no sign of Tim. Don't ask me what happened next or how it happened, but the next thing I knew I was out on Quantuck Bay, floating on the roof of the house I had just left—the telephone pole had crashed into it—and all of the people who had been in the house were with me now, including Tim and the twins. We floated on the bay on that house for the next five hours. We finally landed in the middle of the village at Quogue, behind the Breeze Lawn House, around nine o'clock that night. I went back to Westhampton and got to work, and I didn't get a chance to change my clothes, the same clothes I was wearing when the big wave hit me, until three days later."

*   *   *   *

One of the survivors of the terror on Westhampton Beach was George E. Burghard, who managed to make his way across Moriches Bay during the hurricane on a raftlike piece of wreckage with his wife, Mabel, their two dogs, and a Coastguardman named John Avery. After the storm Burghard, who died in 1963, wrote for his friends a fully detailed account of his ordeal, which gives a vivid picture of the day of the hurricane.

Burghard was an internationally known stamp collector and a radio research engineer who worked closely with Edwin Howard Armstrong on the invention of FM, or frequency-modulation, radio transmission and reception. He rented a large cottage on the ocean side of Westhampton Beach for the summer in 1938, as he had done in previous years, not only because he and his wife enjoyed the beach, but also because the location was ideal for carrying out radio experiments. Burghard installed radio equipment in the cottage and rigged up antennas on the dunes between the cottage and the Coast Guard watch-tower next to it on the west. Mabel Burghard, an attractive blonde woman who proved to be exceptionally calm and fear-less during the hurricane, had been one of America's first woman automobile racing drivers in her youth; in 1918 she had broken the world speed record for women driving a Stutz Bear-cat in a stock-car race. Spending the summer with the Burg-hards at the beach cottage were Carl and Selma Dalin, an elderly couple employed as housekeepers.

Both of the Burghards were tennis fans. They had planned to leave the beach about noon on the day of the hurricane to attend the national singles tennis championships at Forest Hills; they would then stay overnight at their apartment in Man-hattan so that they could meet Burghard's mother when she arrived from Europe the next day. Their next-door neighbors in the cottage east of them on Dune Road, a couple named Livermore, who were also tennis buffs, had left for Forest Hills earlier that morning. But about eleven o'clock Mrs. Burghard learned that the tennis matches had been called off because of the high wind and rain, so they decided to stay at the beach and postpone their trip to the city until the following day. The change in plans pleased Burghard, because he had been watch-

26

ing the storm's strong northeast winds building up during the morning and he loved to watch the surf during a good stiff northeaster. He had spent the previous afternoon with his cousin Bill Ottmann—who was renting a house a half mile to the east on Dune Road—enjoying the spectacle of the surf, which, Burghard said, was higher than he had ever seen it in twenty years of summering at Westhampton. The storm on the day before had been blowing from the south; the winds had died down during the night. Now this new storm was coming in from the northeast, and Burghard was looking forward to another exciting day of watching the surf smash against the high dunes. He talked with Bill Ottmann on the telephone and invited Bill to come over and watch it with him. "This looked like a good northeaster, which was to be expected at that time of year, and caused no concern," Burghard wrote in his chronological account of that momentous day.

One reason why a bad storm caused Burghard little concern was that his rented cottage was unusually well constructed, with concrete foundations and a sturdy wooden bulkhead between it and the ocean surf. It was a solid three-story building behind eight-foot-high dunes. The main living quarters were on the second floor, as is customary in Westhampton Beach oceanfront houses so that their occupants can have a clear view of the ocean over the top of the dunes. On the lower level of the cottage, the level of Dune Road, there were quarters for the servants and a garage with a concrete floor. Burghard was not alarmed—though he might well have been—when Carl Dalin found sea water bubbling up through the concrete in the garage floor about eleven o'clock on the morning of the hurricane day. Although the surf had not yet come over the top of the dunes, it was obviously seeping through them.

Listening to the 1 P.M. news broadcast from New York, Burghard heard the commentator say that the West Indies hurricane that had been off Cape Hatteras seemed to be changing its course and would "probably hit Long Island." The idea of a hurricane on Long Island seemed ridiculous to him. "It was said in such a casual way that I paid no further attention to it," he wrote later. "It seemed impossible anyway. The electric power was still on then."

An hour later there was still no surf coming over the top of the dunes, but the wind had shifted from the northeast to the east and was blowing much harder—about ninety miles per hour, Burghard estimated. He had gone outdoors to secure a dipole antenna and had been knocked down by the force of the wind.

"I managed to get back in the house safely," he wrote. "Then I tried to phone Bill and tell him not to come over, because the wind was so strong that it would blow his car off the road, but the phone was dead. About ten minutes later, he called us and said he wasn't coming because his garage had just blown into the bay."

Mrs. Burghard had been sewing on the sun porch, with her back to the easterly windows. Mrs. Dalin urged her to move to another chair because the windows on the east seemed likely to blow in. She said that she was going to the kitchen anyway, to iron the dress that she had been sewing, and as she stood up, the large window behind her was blown in, filling the sun porch with water and sand. The two men had trouble lashing a door brought up from the basement against the opening of the broken window; the wind was so powerful that they could hardly hold the door in place while they were securing it.

About two thirty in the afternoon, two hours before the

hurricane reached its peak of destruction, Burghard, looking out a window at his battered radio antennas, saw the first wave of the storm rolling across the top of the dunes. It was about four feet deep, and full of force. A few seconds later another wave came over the dunes and carried away the bathhouse and shower fixtures outside his cottage. "This did not look so good," Burghard wrote, "and Mabel said to me, 'Don't you think it's getting serious?' I didn't know what to say. She had gotten wet from the rain coming through the broken window, and had gone upstairs to put on her bathing suit, which proved very useful later."

The servants' quarters and the garage on the lower floor of the cottage were now flooded with three feet of water. Burghard asked Dalin to go below and to bring some clothing upstairs to the third-floor guest room, where he and his wife could spend the night. Then he went outside to the lee, or west, side of the cottage to try to take down some of his antennas. As he came out of the house from the basement, another big wave washed over the dunes and he had to grasp one of the antenna poles to keep from being washed to Dune Road.

While Burghard was struggling with the antennas he saw John Avery, the Coastguardman who was on duty alone at the nearby watchtower, wading toward him across the churning white surf. Avery warned him that he and his wife and the Dalins had to get out of their cottage and try somehow to make their way across the bay to the mainland. It was then about 3:30. Burghard realized that high tide that day was scheduled for 6:10 P.M. "If the tide is this high now," he said to himself, "what will it be like at 6:10?"

"We went into the house and everyone was quite calm, no trace of panic," Burghard wrote in his account of the storm.

"Avery said we would have to leave the house and walk to the bridge, one half mile to the east. This was our best chance, as even if we couldn't make it across the bridge, the bay narrows down there to one hundred feet or more, which would be only a short swim at the most, while from where we were it was well over a mile across to the mainland. I told the Dalins we would have to abandon ship, and gave the old man a pair of boots; then sent Mabel upstairs to put on some shoes, as the walking was very dangerous on account of the wreckage.

"The surf was now running through the bottom of the house, all white water. I went up to the bedroom on the third floor to see what I could find to take along. Mabel did likewise and put on a pair of sandals. Strange things happen in extraordinary circumstances. Mabel took a pair of lorgnettes, put them around her neck, and put her handbag on her arm. I looked at my watch on the night table and some cuff links, disregarded them entirely, never thought of my keys, but found two season tickets for the tennis matches at Forest Hills. I immediately thought to myself, 'I must have these because I want to see the semifinals tomorrow,' and put them in my trousers pocket. That, strange as it may seem, was the only thing I tried to save."

Downstairs Burghard found the Dalins fearful and hesitant about leaving the cottage. Mrs. Dalin, trying to busy herself in the kitchen, asked, "Do we really have to go?" Dalin said, "Can't I take my car?" His new car, which Burghard had given him earlier in the summer, was his pride and joy. Burghard explained to them that all of them had to leave the house at once because it was in danger of caving in, and that trying to take a car was useless, not only because the engine had been soaked in sea water but because the waves would wash a car off the road.

Mabel Burghard came downstairs, put a leather jacket on over her bathing suit, which she had bought in Hawaii and cherished, and decided that she and her husband would carry their two beloved dogs; she took Peter, the cocker spaniel, and Burghard followed her with Bitzie, the wire-haired fox terrier. At the door of the garage, the only exit from the cottage, they found themselves up to their waists in foaming surf water and unable to open the door. Avery, who had been trying to hurry the reluctant Dalins, came down the stairs and helped Burghard open the door and jam it into place. Then the Burghards with their dogs floundered outside into the swirling surf on the driveway, while Avery went back to urge on the terrified Dalins, who wanted no part of the storm outdoors.

Dune Road, as Burghard described it later, was a roaring torrent filled with pieces of lumber from wrecked houses. The Burghards made their way east to the fence and hedge in front of the Livermore house next door, which gave them a little protection from surf that was washing against them from the dunes. They placed the two dogs in the hedge and waited for Avery and the two Dalins to come out of their cottage to join them.

Finally Avery appeared, dragging Mrs. Dalin to the hedge where the Burghards were waiting. "She was terribly frightened, and Mabel tried to comfort her by telling her to grab a telegraph pole, which she did," Burghard recalled later. "I looked back and saw Carl Dalin walk out of the driveway, get to a fence post on the road behind our house, and sit down. He was only seventy-five feet west of where we were all together. We called to him, since he was to the leeward and could have heard, but he never even moved his head—just sat there with his head down, looking at the water. Of course, time was getting short, so Avery and I worked Mrs. Dalin loose from the pole, after much trouble, and started to walk east."

It was then that the wind shifted around to the south, bringing the main brute force of the hurricane waves smashing over the narrow beach and roaring into the wild bay.

"Green waves, some fifty feet high, came over and the surf began breaking right on top of us," Burghard wrote. "We managed to resist the first of it, but then had to get hold of the telephone poles to duck the wreckage. Mabel, with her short legs, was down a few times but we managed to haul her out, and the dogs, by some miracle, stayed in the hedge. Mrs. Dalin became absolutely hysterical and dragged Avery and myself to another pole—nearer her husband, who never moved—and took a death grip on the pole, screaming and yelling."

Avery and the Burghards decided that trying to walk east toward the bridge and the narrower part of the bay was impossible; their only hope of survival, they agreed, was to swim across the bay from where they were standing, even though the bay there was almost a mile wide. The two men kicked off their boots, threw off their coats, and cut off the legs of their long trousers with a penknife. Mabel Burghard stripped down to her bathing suit, removing her leather jacket and her sandals, but kept her lorgnette around her neck and her handbag on her arm.

Burghard noticed that a small rowboat, belonging to his absent neighbors, the Livermores, was still tied to their dock on the bay side of Dune Road; their large cabin cruiser had been carried away from its mooring about noon. Burghard had a wild notion of putting the Dalins into the rowboat and sending them off across the bay in it. He made a run for the boat, but just as he was about to reach for it the rope tying it to the dock "snapped like a violin string," and the little boat raced away from him across the bay.

Fighting his way back to his wife and Avery and the panic-stricken Dalins, Burghard saw the nearby Coast Guard station smashed into pieces without a noise that he could hear; its steel lookout tower and one-hundred-foot radio mast toppled over and were washed into the bay. Like most people who watched such destruction during the hurricane, he was astonished by its apparent soundlessness. The high velocity of the wind submerged other noises. "The effect was that of a silent movie," he said. Seeing the Coast Guard tower collapse, Burghard wondered if it would knock down electric power lines on Dune Road and throw an electric charge into the waist-high water, electrocuting everybody near it on the beach. He yelled a warning. Later he realized that his fear was silly because electric power on the beach and on most of the Long Island mainland had been cut off hours before.

The Burghards and Avery decided to go to the Livermore dock, which was then still standing intact, and to lie down flat on it, hoping that a big wave from the ocean would wash the dock, with them on it, into the bay. They called to the Dalins to follow them. Mrs. Dalin was still holding tightly to the telephone pole and screaming. Dalin was in the same position—sitting beside the fence post—that he had taken after leaving the cottage. He was not looking at his wife or at anybody else; he still had his head bowed, staring at the water swirling around his chest. The Burghards decided to abandon their two dogs, placing them again on the hedge, but Peter, the small cocker spaniel, looked so sad and helpless that George Burghard tucked him under one arm, using his other arm to support his wife. When they reached the dock, they discovered that Bitzie, the fox terrier, had left the hedge and joined them, swimming most of the way. Again the Burghards and Avery called to the Dalins to follow them. "We felt sure that this couldn't last much longer," Burghard wrote, "and that when we got over to the mainland we could come back in a boat and get them. It never occurred to us that this was a major catastrophe." In other words, like most of the victims of the hurricane, they assumed that the storm was a disturbance affecting only their immediate area.

While the Burghards and Avery were waiting for the dock to be washed across the bay, they saw the large bathhouse beside the Livermore cottage breaking up. A flat piece of the structure came floating toward them and they grabbed it. Mabel Burghard, remaining calm, jumped into a sitting position with the two dogs in the center of the makeshift raft; Avery was on one end of it and George Burghard on the other. They sat there waiting for the next high wave from the ocean to carry them into the bay, as one soon did.

The powerful wind had driven most of the water in the bay across to the mainland and up into estuaries and creeks and boat canals, flooding lowlands and marshes in some places as far north as beyond the Montauk Highway. Much of the bay bottom was left dry and exposed, except when a new big wave would roll in across the barrier beach from the ocean, bringing a rolling flood of white surf, five or six feet deep, which would rush across the mud flats for a few hundred feet before it subsided. The Burghards and their companion from the Coast Guard station were carried out into the middle of the mile-wide bay by a series of these waves, which would pick up their raft and carry them forward for a while, then drop them temporarily on the muddy bottom to wait for the next lift from the rush of new surf.

They found themselves followed and surrounded by dangerous wreckage with protruding nails and by smashed bodies of automobiles. At one point, Burghard noted, a huge black fuel tank, fifty feet long and ten feet wide, came after them, "bobbing up and down on the waves like a sea monster," but it missed them. Doors and large planks flew high above their heads in the gusts of hurricane gales. Like their raft, the bodies of automobiles and the large hunks of debris from wrecked houses would be picked up and thrown forward by the waves, and then dropped on the bay bottom until they were finally carried into the deep water farther out, where they sank.

When the Burghard-Avery raft reached the deep water of the bay it began to sink, no doubt because it had been shaken so hard by the jolting series of jumps across the shallow stretch nearer the ocean beach. The waves in the bay also became higher and more powerful as the water became deeper. (That day the navigation channel in the middle of Moriches Bay must have been filled with hurricane-swept water as deep as forty feet.) Now and then Mabel Burghard would be washed off the raft. Her husband would stretch his foot over the side for her to grasp until he could reach for her with his hands and pull her back on board. As the water rose over the surface of the sinking raft, Bitzie, the lively fox terrier, climbed up on the back of Mabel's neck to escape from it and more than once pushed her head under the water. The men salvaged from some floating wreckage a slab of wood that could provide the two dogs with a raft of their own, placed them on it, and shoved them off.

When they had floated about one hundred feet ahead of the other refugees, they both jumped from their raft and swam back to the Burghards against gales of more than one hundred miles per hour.

Holding on to the raft became still more difficult as it sank deeper in the higher waves, and sometimes all three of the passengers and the two dogs would be swept off together. The dogs would scramble back to the raft carrying sticks in their mouths and would drop them in the Burghards' laps, as if the whole grim voyage was a game. "All this helped to maintain mental equilibrium," Burghard wrote. "Once Bitzie fell off, and Peter jumped right in after him, and swam back towing him by the ear. Courageous little guy, that!"

Mrs. Burghard was later quoted by a *New York Times* reporter as saying that the bay had been full of screaming people, but her husband in his written account noted that he had not seen another living person between the time they left the ocean beach and the time they floated near the mainland shore at the Oneck Point section of Westhampton.

"To add to the awesome feeling of drifting in the semidarkness, with wreckage all around us and pieces of wood flying by, driven by the terrible wind, was the absolute absence of humanity," Burghard wrote. "It was very difficult to reconcile ourselves to the fact that there were no rescue boats coming out to meet us, but of course no boats could have made any headway against that wind and such waves. Just as our faithful raft was going down for the third time, along came a large piece of a house, well studded with nails but flat. Avery and I grabbed it, and he said somebody ought to get onto that, and lighten the load. So I, being the heaviest, climbed over and found it so large that Mabel and Avery both came aboard with the pups.

This was really a nice raft, and for the first time since we left the beach, we could sit up above water, which was a great relief. There was even a place where we could brace our feet and hold on, so the waves couldn't wash us off any more.

"We were now beyond the channel and the danger of wreckage piling on top of us was very great. Great parts of houses with spikes sticking out were chasing us on every hand. Avery and I each picked up a long board and with the aid of these managed to push ourselves around all the big pieces as the waves piled them up on us. It was quite a job, but by paddling and pushing we managed to get between all the houses, roofs . . . and let them go by."

A flock of wild ducks appeared in the west. Burghard pretended to shoot at them with his board. His wife joined Avery in laughing at him, although she thought at the time, as she told him later, that he was cracking up and going crazy.

When the Burghards and Avery left the ocean beach, the hurricane winds had been blowing from the southeast, driving their raft westward on Moriches Bay, where they could have drifted for many hours before reaching the shore. Luckily, as the cyclonic storm moved in closer to Long Island and passed over, the wind shifted to the south and then swung around toward the southwest, turning their raft north toward the closer Oneck Point shore, near the golf course of the Westhampton Country Club.

"There was a house on the point, just west of Oneck, and it looked as if we were going to land there," Burghard wrote. "When we were still out in the bay about three hundred yards, we saw people on the front porch, about ten of them. This was a welcome sight, and we thought surely they had seen us and were waiting with a drink and blankets to warm us up. We all

37

waved to them with a great feeling of relief, but not one of them responded. They just kept milling about on the porch, which was well under water. . . . The wind and the waves swept us on, and we finally grounded in a clump of berry bushes about fifty feet from the house. We looked for the people we had seen on the porch but to our great disappointment they had all disappeared. No one was in sight to give us a hand—we were all alone again."

Avery and Burghard helped Mrs. Burghard from the raft, and Peter, the cocker spaniel, jumped into the three feet of water in the bushes and followed her. Bitzie, the fox terrier, jumped to another floating piece of debris and disappeared in the bushes about one hundred feet away. Burghard and the others searched for the terrier but he was not to be found. Having given up the search, the Burghards and Avery made their way out of the bushes and the piled-up debris to an expanse of clear and high ground, which they recognized as the eleventh fairway of the Westhampton Country Club golf course. "Peter joined us, tickled to death to be on dry land; so were we," Burghard said. They were also glad to be in the open space of the golf course fairway because the gale was still blowing hard and trees were still falling in nearby wooded areas.

A woman came out of the apparently empty house near their landing place and waded through the water to where they were standing. The woman was hysterical and not making much sense, but they gathered that she was trying to tell them that two babies were stranded in the house. Avery told the Burghards to go to the village for shelter and warmth, and left them to go back to the house with the woman to help the children.

The Burghards walked along the golf course for about two miles; they had little sense of direction until they reached the main road between Westhampton and Remsenburg, which was familiar to them.

"As we walked along we took account of ourselves," Burghard wrote. "Mabel had on just the bathing suit. The lorgnettes were still around her neck, and her handbag, dripping water, was still on her arm, with cruel welts showing where the handle had bruised her flesh. We were both in our bare feet; I with just the remains of a pair of trousers, and our legs bruised and bleeding from many cuts and scratches but nothing broken, although Mabel's ankle and wrist were badly swollen. I had Mabel by the arm but the wind was so strong that several times she was taken right off her feet and I had to pull her back by the wrist. Peter was running about having a grand time. The darkness seemed to lift and the sun tried to come through the clouds. The rain had stopped entirely but the wind was chilling us to the bone."

About a mile from Westhampton village, the Burghards were stopped by a wide, roaring torrent of water in a low dip in the road where they had never seen water before. A telephone company truck tried to pass through the flood from the opposite side of it, but stalled in the middle of the torrent with water above its wheels.

"There we were, half-naked, shivering and bleeding, but nobody paid any attention to us," Burghard wrote. "A car drove up beside us. The driver never even looked at us, and a woman came out of a nearby house and also paid no attention to us. Apparently in disasters of this kind everyone is so frightened and worried that they have no time for anyone else. The man got out of the car and came over to us as though we were sight-seers and said, 'How can I get to Westhampton? Can I get through here?' I said, 'No, you can't, but if you are going to Westhampton, we'll go with you.' We opened the door and hopped in, dog and all. He turned around and told us he was looking for his family and had been two hours trying to get into Westhampton. His name was McKnight, and a very nice chap. We tried road after road but they were all blocked by trees and telephone poles, which were still falling. At last we came to Montauk Highway and then found a way into Westhampton. We stopped at Perry's drug store, which is east of the town on Main Street. We got out. There was no one in sight, and in the center of town there was at least six feet of swirling water, which was still rising. I said, 'O.K., thanks for the lift. We'll go to Perry's and get warm.' We walked to the drug store and found it closed tight and deserted. The rain had started again, and with the terrific wind, was chilling us badly.

"Just then a man walked by, leading an old lady. I called to him, 'Where can we get warm?' He said, 'Follow me to the Howell House; it has a stove.' So, beachcombers that we were, we followed him across to the Howell House, the summer hotel which had closed for the season that morning. Due to the storm, they had opened it up again. As we walked in with the dog, Peter, and our bleeding legs, bare feet, and scant clothing, the people there just looked at us and said, 'What do you want?' We said, 'Where can we get warm? We just swam across the bay.' They looked at us skeptically, which I can well understand, as everyone was so frightened that they thought it was the end of Long Island, and the water was still rising. Finally someone took us into the kitchen, and there we stayed before the coal range, where they brought us coffee and brandy, and we were really warmed up."

While the Burghards huddled beside the kitchen stove with other storm refugees who were worried about the rising sea water on the main street, Mabel Burghard caused consternation by announcing that the whole of Long Island was probably sinking. Such a catastrophe had been predicted two years earlier, she said. Burghard figured later that when he and his wife arrived at the Howell House it was about six o'clock, the time of that day's high tide, which undoubtedly caused the high rise of water in the center of the town. A half hour later the flood on Main Street began to recede and everybody felt relieved and less nervous about the future of Long Island. The manager of the hotel provided the Burghards with dry clothing, sandwiches, and drinks, and treated their wounds with disinfectants.

Burghard was anxious to find out what had happened to the Dalins and to learn whether Bill Ottmann and his family had escaped safely from the beach. He left his wife at the Howell House and walked to Main Street, where he was stopped by an armed guard who was protecting stores against looters. At the village police station, Burghard had his name and that of his wife removed from the list of missing persons, which at that hour still included the Dalins and the Ottmanns. At the Patio Restaurant, he found Jack Face, Bill Ottmann's chauffeur, who assured him that Bill and his family were safe, and asleep. "This was a great relief, so we all had a drink," Burghard wrote.

But later in the night Burghard identified the body of Carl Dalin at the clubhouse of the Westhampton Country Club, which had been turned into a temporary morgue. Dalin's body had been washed ashore on the golf course near the place where the Burghards and Avery had landed. Identifying him was a gruesome ordeal, Burghard said, because there were no electric or oil lights in the clubhouse and each of the recovered bodies had to be examined with a flashlight. At five o'clock the next morning Selma Dalin's body, which had been picked up on the bay shore a half mile from where her husband had been found, was identified among another group of dead people at a local funeral home.

A few hours later, in bright and warm sunshine, the Burghards drove to New York City with the Ottmanns, "glad to be alive and considering ourselves very lucky." Later in the week, Burghard learned that his beach cottage and that of the Livermores to the east had both been completely swept away by the hurricane waves after he and his wife and Avery had left the Livermore dock. The dunes were so flattened that both sites were under water at high tide for months after the storm. A few feet east of the Livermore cottage a new inlet, two hundred feet wide and fourteen feet deep, had been cut through the beach from the ocean to the bay.

"After many days of searching, we found practically nothing of value," Burghard wrote. "The roof and attic of our house was washed up in a swale behind the first hole of the Westhampton golf course, about three miles from where it started. The largest radio pole with halyards intact was found right on the first green of the golf course, and a vest from one of my suits was nearby, twenty feet up in a tree. We found both of Mabel's riding boots, one at least a half mile from the other. One of my slippers was perched near a Coast Guard lifeboat a mile inland. Incidentally, there was a piece of shingle driven through the side of this boat with the force of a rifle bullet."

Mabel Burghard died in 1960, three years before the death of her husband. "As brave as my mother was during the hurricane," says Mrs. Albert K. Trout, Jr., of Coconut Grove, Florida, Mrs. Burghard's daughter from a previous marriage, "I don't think she ever quite recovered from the horrifying experience for the rest of her life." Recently Mrs. Trout supplied two interesting postscripts to George Burghard's story.

"I have with me down here in Florida his dipole antenna from Westhampton Beach," Mrs. Trout wrote. "There is a plaque on it, presented to the Burghards that following Christmas by Edwin Howard Armstrong, the inventor of FM radio, and Randy Runyon, another great old-time radio man, and the inscription on the plaque reads as follows:

THIS DIPOLE ANTENNA TOGETHER WITH ITS REFLECTOR

WAS THE ONLY PIECE OF RADIO EQUIPMENT RECOVERED

FROM THE WESTHAMPTON BEACH STATION OF

GEORGE EHRET BURGHARD

AFTER THE HURRICANE OF SEPT 21, 1938

IT WAS FOUND INTACT IN THE ROOF OF THE BUILDING

A MILE INLAND ACROSS MORICHES BAY. THE OWNER

OF THE ANTENNA AND HIS WIFE SWAM THE BAY DURING

THE HURRICANE

EVEN HURRICANES DO NOT STOP THE OLD TIMERS

MERRY CHRISTMAS 1938

HOWARD AND RANDY

"The other thing concerns Bitzie, the frisky little wire-haired fox terrier who disappeared after they landed in the bushes at Oneck Point. Bitzie remained among the missing for a whole year after the hurricane. Then one day, a year later, he turned up at Westhampton Beach and the police returned him to the surprised and delighted Burghards. He lived with them happily for the rest of his life, which was a long one for a dog, because he didn't die until he was sixteen years old."

43

Not many of the people who survived the bewildering terror of the hurricane at Westhampton Beach remembered it later with such total recall as that of George Burghard. One of the few survivors who remained on the ocean beach during the whole storm—and endured the worst of it out of doors, huddled beside a fortunately high and strong sand dune—was the then twenty-one-year-old Joan Schmid, now Mrs. Walter J. Coleman of Islip, Long Island. Her recollection of the long day and night on the beach has blank spots that now puzzle her. She has trouble, for example, remembering the other people who were with her on the sand dune at the height of the storm and who spent the night with her in a battered cottage nearby after the wind and waves subsided.

"Perhaps I was more dazed and shocked than I realized at the time," Mrs. Coleman said recently. "That may have been the reason, too, why all of us in the group I was with remained so amazingly calm during and after the storm. That I do remember clearly, how calm we all were. I wasn't thinking much about myself. In a situation like that, you think of other people, not only those around you but more particularly the ones who were with you an hour or so ago and who are now missing. The worst part of the whole experience for me was not the storm itself but the week after it—going to all those funerals of close friends whom we had been with . . . that day."

On the day of the hurricane Joan's parents, Mr. and Mrs. John H. Schmid, of Brooklyn, were attending a wedding in the city, having left her and her younger sister, Mona, now Mrs. Carroll Cavanagh of East Norwalk, Connecticut, at their summer beach cottage with the family's two maids. About noon

Joan and Mona decided to drive west on Dune Road to visit their close friend Peggy Connolly Brown, twenty-one-year-old wife of Peter Campbell Brown, a New York lawyer. Mrs. Brown was sitting out the storm in her oceanfront cottage with her seven-month-old daughter, Judith, and a maid; her husband was at work in the city. "I remember that I was wearing my diamond bracelet that morning," Joan said. "My mother was always joshing me about getting all dressed up with jewelry even when I was going out to buy a newspaper, so I took the bracelet off before we went out to drive to Peggy's. I never saw it again, and that was the last diamond bracelet I ever owned. We also had a lot of new clothes in our cottage that we had bought at the late-season sales in the Southampton shops and had never worn. That went, too."

The two sisters drove in their family's big and heavy La Salle sedan along Dune Road to the Brown cottage without paying much attention to the storm, which, they assumed, was one of the usual September northeasters. "We still didn't pay much attention to what was going on outside while we were with Peggy and her baby at her cottage," Joan said. "Not until about three thirty, when the telephone rang, and it was Annie Seeley, one of our maids, calling me to tell me that our house was collapsing and its roof was blowing off. Annie was badly frightened. While I was trying to talk with her and calm her down, the phone went dead. How the phone was working at all up to that point, I don't know. Apparently it was still connected right up until our house was washed away."

The two Schmid girls hurried to their car to drive back to their cottage to help Annie Seeley, not realizing that the cottage had already been destroyed and that Annie had been drowned in the bay. They urged Peggy Brown and her maid to go with them, but Peggy was reluctant to carry her baby outside into the heavy wind and rain, so she and her maid stayed behind. As Joan and Mona were driving slowly through the water and blinding spray and blowing sand on Dune Road, they saw another friend, Mrs. Kathryn Bragaw, and her eighteen-year-old daughter, Carolyn, waving and beckoning to them from the door of the Bragaw cottage. The Bragaws were apparently inviting them to leave their car and come inside for shelter, but Joan and Mona were too worried about Annie Seeley to stop. They drove on eastward toward their home.

"As it turned out, that frantic phone call from Annie saved our lives," Joan recalled recently. "The Brown cottage was later washed away, and so was the Bragaw cottage. Peggy and her baby and her maid, and Mrs. Bragaw and Carolyn, were all killed. Peggy's body wasn't found until several days later, on the ocean side of the beach at Southampton. Her baby was never found. If Mona and I had not been so worried about Annie, we certainly would have stayed with Peggy at her house or we might have stopped on Dune Road and gone into the Bragaws' house. Then we would have been killed, too. But we kept on trying to get to poor Annie, and that was what saved us."

Before they could reach their house, or the site where it had been, their car stalled in the rising water on Dune Road. They got out and tried to walk the rest of the way, but trying to walk against the fierce gale and the waist-high surf rushing over the dunes was impossible. The two girls saw one high dune on the ocean side of the road that was standing firm against the wild surf. On the sandy slope of the dune was an old and apparently long-abandoned rowboat, which would be something to cling to if the dune was washed away. Joan and Mona made their way to the dune and crouched on the sand beside the boat, which gave them a little protection against the wind. Their car was never seen again.

Soon the girls were joined on the dune by six other refugees, two maids with the twenty-one-month-old son of the family for whom they worked, and an elderly crippled man who had been dragged across the sand and surf by his sister and his chauffeur. The small child, later identified in the newspapers as Arthur H. Brook, had been left in the care of the two maids, Irene Mitkowski and Helen Diorzan, at the nearby Brook cottage while his mother had gone on a shopping trip. "We sat there on the dune, watching the water climbing closer and closer toward our feet," Joan said. "Mona and I prayed. We said many Acts of Contrition. Finally, we noticed that the water wasn't rising any higher and the wind seemed to be dying down a little. We decided that the worst of the storm was probably over."

The badly battered Brook cottage was one of the few houses remaining on the beach after the storm subsided; it was as wet and broken inside from the flooding surf as it was on the outside. The group on the dune, led by Irene Mitkowski, the Brook family's nursemaid, made their way to the cottage and took shelter there for the night. The two maids found candles in the house and kept them lighted in a window during the night, hoping to attract a rescue party from the mainland. Early in the morning they were spotted by a Coast Guard patrol boat, and later the group was picked up by one of the privately owned motorboats that had been drafted for rescue work. Joan remembered walking into the center of Westhampton village in her bare feet, which were swollen and sore from poison ivy infection, and being stopped by a woman who gave her a pair of men's thick woolen socks. At the Patio Restaurant, where a crowd of refugees were assembled, Joan and Mona were urged to swallow, for the first time in their lives, a drink of whiskey. The girls went to the telephone company building, the only place in town where a telephone call could be made to New York City and other parts of Long Island, to make an attempt to reach their parents or other relatives. Despite the hurricane devastation, the New York Telephone Company was not providing free service, and Joan had to borrow some money from a friend to pay for her calls. Unable to contact her parents in the city, because they were driving to Westhampton to look for her and Mona, Joan managed to get through a call to her married older sister, Miriam Lessing, at Bayport, a town sixteen miles west of Westhampton on Great South Bay where there had been comparatively little storm damage. When Joan assured Miriam that she and Mona were safe and unhurt after being stranded on the beach during the hurricane, Miriam could not understand at first what she was talking about. Communications on Long Island had been so blacked out that Miriam, only sixteen miles away, did not know that Westhampton Beach had been destroyed by the hurricane the day before.

"My father and mother got into Westhampton that afternoon and found us, and we drove back to the city that night," Joan recalled recently. "On the way, we stopped at Bayport and visited Miriam and her husband, Larry Lessing. I remember that while we were sitting and talking about the storm, I found myself leaning over to my right side as I sat on my chair. Without realizing it, I was still trying to lean against the wind to keep myself from being blown over, as I had done on the dune at the beach during the storm."

* * * *

48

At the peak of the hurricane, when the wind at Westhampton Beach was blowing from the south, the wind at the Fire Island community of Saltaire—thirty-five miles to the west on the same stretch of barrier beach, but slightly on the opposite side of the hurricane's eye—was blowing from the northwest, against the ocean surf instead of from it. Despite the offshore direction of the revolving cyclonic gales on this west side of the hurricane, the storm waves from the ocean at Saltaire and its neighboring summer colony of Kismet were almost as high and destructive as those at Westhampton Beach; the surf on the bay side of the beach was, of course, wilder. Saltaire was badly beaten by the hurricane: a break-through of water from the ocean to the bay was torn across the middle of the settlement, and seventy-five cottages were broken up or washed away. Like most of the Fire Island summer colonies, Saltaire had few casualties because most of its cottages had been closed for the season after Labor Day; only three of the seventy-five people on the beach during the storm were drowned. But for one group of five people, two women and a married couple and their four-year-old son, who were trapped on the ocean side of the Saltaire beach, the hurricane was a terrifying experience. One of the women, Elsie Overton, wrote a letter about their ordeal, which was later preserved in a mimeographed history of Saltaire.

Mrs. Overton was staying at the oceanfront cottage of her brother, William P. Corbett, with a woman companion whom she referred to in her letter as "B." Most of the houses on the ocean dunes around the Corbett cottage had been closed for the winter. Mrs. Overton's only near neighbors were a couple whom she referred to as Mr. and Mrs. H. and their four-year-old son. About three thirty on the afternoon of the hurricane, Mrs. Overton and her friend were forced to flee from her brother's cottage because massive waves were washing over it. "As we fled," she wrote, "a wave now estimated at thirty feet high came roaring after us, carrying the remnants of the wooden crosswalks we were on with it, plunging us into water and washing us to the closed cottage behind us. Mr. and Mrs. H. were there, calling to us to help them break in the door. Their own cottage opposite had already broken up and was floating away in pieces. No sooner had we gotten inside, through broken glass, than this cottage began to break up around us. The refrigerator, the stove, and furniture piled up on us. Windows blew in and water rose to our waists. We climbed a ladder through a trap door to the pitch-black attic. There was no exit to the roof, and even if we could have gotten out and tried clinging to the chimney, we would have been swept off the roof by the wind and the water washing over it.

"We huddled at the opening of the attic, frozen and wet, and watched the water below rise to our hanging feet. The floor of the attic only consisted of crossbeams, so we could not stand on it to get higher above the water. We knew the tide would continue to rise for two more hours, and not one of us four adults expected that we would get out of that trap alive. It is strange what resignation you feel at a time like that. The little boy was a wonderful sport, frightened, of course, but worrying more about his Teddy bear and the kittens he had left behind. His mother sang to him, and confided to me that when the final crash came, she would hold his head under the water so that he might drown quickly before being injured by the force of the waves and the wreckage."

Having resigned themselves to death, the three women and the man in the attic could hardly believe their eyes when they saw the water below them receding a few hours later. They climbed down the ladder and discovered that the cottage had been carried three quarters of a mile across the beach, from its lot on the ocean dunes to the shore of the bay, where it had lodged beside a fallen telephone pole, half in and half out of the water. They picked up a box of crackers, a package of apricots, a can of soup, and a carton of cigarettes that they found in the kitchen and went outside, wading through water and debris.

The little group found themselves separated from the center of the village and its ferry dock by the newly cut inlet from the ocean to the bay, which was filled with rushing water. They decided not to take the chance of trying to cross the inlet in the darkness of the night, and elected to spend the night in a nearby bayside cottage, which Mrs. Overton recognized as the home of a grocer. There they found coffee and a half bottle of water, from which they made hot coffee, and candles, which they lighted and waved in the windows as signals. During the night they took turns signaling and trying to rest and keep warm in the beds. Only the little boy managed to fall asleep. The group also changed into dry clothes that they found in the grocer's cottage. "I put on the grocer's large brown sneakers, a long pink evening slip tucked into a pair of bright blue denim trousers with red stripes on the seams, and a white peekaboo sweater from which I burst the buttons in my haste," Mrs. Overton wrote.

In the morning they saw people on the ferry dock, where the Saltaire ferry was pinned down in debris. The only escape from that end of Fire Island was by boat, so most of the people at Saltaire had gathered on the ferry and on another boat at the dock during the storm, but the two boats had been unable to move into the bay because of the wreckage piled around them. The people had therefore spent the night in the town hall. Heads had been counted, and when Mrs. Overton and her friend were discovered missing, a group of men had gone to their ocean-front cottage to search for them at three o'clock in the morning. Later, when Mrs. Overton and her companions left the grocer's cottage and waded across the new inlet to the ferry dock, "men came running to embrace us, simply astonished that we were alive and unharmed."

In their makeshift costumes from the grocer's closet, Mrs. Overton and her friend were taken in a private boat to the Long Island mainland at Bay Shore, where an elderly gentleman, having volunteered to help the refugees, took them to a hotel, the Cortland House, in his chauffeur-driven limousine. There Mrs. Overton talked to reporters from New York, and was somewhat annoyed by the quotations attributed to her in the newspapers the next day.

"I did not 'go up into the attic to pray,' as the New York *Post* reported," she wrote in her letter. "Nor did I say that our cottage 'was impaled on a telegraph pole like an Eskimo Pie,' although it was a very apt description."

*   *   *   *

The inland and north-shore villages on the east end of Long Island, spared from the ocean waves during the hurricane, suffered heavy damage from the gales that blew in gusts well over one hundred miles per hour. In the old whaling village of Sag Harbor, a gust of wind picked up the tall steeple of the Presbyterian church, a landmark for fishermen for more than a century, and lifted the whole tower structure in one piece. With its bell tolling sadly, it was carried twenty feet away from the church building and then dropped. The steeple crashed on the ground without touching the rest of the church, which remained undamaged.

As George Burghard noted, such destruction during the hurricane seemed to be noiseless. "It was like watching an explosion or a train wreck on television with the sound turned off," another man who was in the storm said not long ago. "You could see a house across the street from you falling apart, but you couldn't hear it." Apparently the high-pitched scream of the gales was so intense and constant that few other sounds could rise above it. The people who saw the steeple on the Presbyterian church in Sag Harbor being lifted and dropped say that it crashed on the ground without any noise, but they remember hearing its bell. The ringing of the bell must have been vibrant enough to penetrate the din of the gales, but the crash of the steeple seemed silent.

On Long Island, as elsewhere later, the hurricane performed strange tricks. Leaves of trees were stripped cleanly from the stems, while the stems stayed firmly attached to their branches. Pieces of flat boards and blunt sticks of wood were driven through walls of houses by the gales. Many chickens had their feathers plucked completely by the wind. A cow pastured before the storm on an island in Moriches Bay was found later, safe and sound, in a thicket three quarters of a mile away on the mainland. Herman Schoenfeld's cottage at Cherry Grove on Fire Island was picked up by a wave and carried two hundred yards to a location formerly occupied by another cottage. There the Schoenfeld cottage was completely turned around and placed upright. The lamps on the tables were undisturbed and a jug of water in the kitchen sink remained right side up without a drop having been spilled from it. Not far away on the same wrecked beach, a fresh egg, whole and uncracked, was found resting gently on a pile of debris from a smashed kitchen. Many trees that were bent downward and partly uprooted by the first blow of the hurricane were later raised back upright and restored to their original straight positions when the wind shifted to the opposite direction after the lull in the middle of the storm.

*   *   *   *

In New York City, on the milder west side of the cyclonic circle, the storm was not officially regarded as a hurricane because the gales did not sustain a force of seventy-five miles per hour. But late in the afternoon thousands of workers were trapped in office buildings after working hours because the winds were blowing at sixty-eight miles per hour—with gusts much higher than hurricane intensity—making the streets unsafe for pedestrians and stopping traffic. Two hundred and fifty flat-bottomed rowboats from the lakes at Central Park were rushed to Queens for emergency rescue duty when the streets of that borough were flooded. The East River rose more than six feet above extreme high-tide level and covered North Brother Island completely, extinguishing electric power at Riverside Hospital.

The French Line's *Ile de France* arrived in New York Harbor from Europe at the height of the storm. A Coast Guard cutter that went out to meet the ship at quarantine, carrying a pilot, customs officers, and news reporters, was unable to find it in the thick rain and mist. When the *Ile de France* appeared out of the fog in the Hudson River, it was listing sharply to starboard in the fierce gales and had to be pushed into its pier by twelve tugboats instead of the usual six. The *Queen Mary*, scheduled to sail from its West 50th Street pier at four thirty that afternoon, had its departure postponed until the next morning because of the hurricane. The 968 passengers were told that they could go ashore for the night, but less than one hundred of them left the ship. *Bon voyage* parties went on in the staterooms until the small hours of the morning. New York City suffered more than five million dollars in damages during the hurricane, and ten deaths were reported.

There was heavy wind and flood damage in Westchester County, and high waves from the hurricane, rolling ashore suddenly and unexpectedly, caused widespread destruction all along the New Jersey coast. At Atlantic City and Asbury Park, miles of boardwalk were ripped up and swept as much as three street blocks inland, smashing houses along the way. At the seaside resort of Loch Arbor in New Jersey, a New Yorker named Edgar Foulks, standing on a bulkhead in front of his oceanside summer cottage, was picked up from it and swept bodily inland for a long distance by a towering storm wave. When the wave receded, its undertow carried Foulks back again to the bulkhead and threw him against it. He suffered only a few bruises, but his wife, who had watched his disappearance and reappearance from the nearby cottage, had to be taken to a hospital because she was in a state of shock. In Bayonne, New Jersey, George Buettner came out of his house after the storm and saw a broken wire draped across the top of his parked automobile. He tried to brush it aside with his left hand and was electrocuted instantly.

The horse racing at Belmont Park in Queens went on as scheduled despite the storm, but the feature race of the day, the Westchester Claiming Stakes over six furlongs on the old Widener straightaway course, was not timed. The rain was so thick that the timer at the finish line could not see the drop of the starter's flag.

3

FROM LONG ISLAND, the center of the hurricane moved north into the middle of Connecticut, spreading so much destruction that the Hartford *Courant* mourned September 21, 1938, as the "most calamitous day" in the state's history. "As nearly as the crippled communications can indicate," the *Courant* said after the storm, "no community of any size escaped damage. New Haven is still dark and battered. The heart of New London is in smoking ruins. Along the shore, the combination of an extraordinarily high tide, described by some witnesses as a tidal wave, and hurricane winds has left behind a shambles of broken trees, shattered houses, and smashed boats. On not a major highway in Connecticut has traffic moved unimpeded. Estimates of the cost in lives and property are pure guesswork, for it will be days before complete reports can be compiled. Together, fire, wind, and flood have made a day of black catastrophe."

The day of the hurricane would have been even blacker if Connecticut's geographical situation had not been relatively

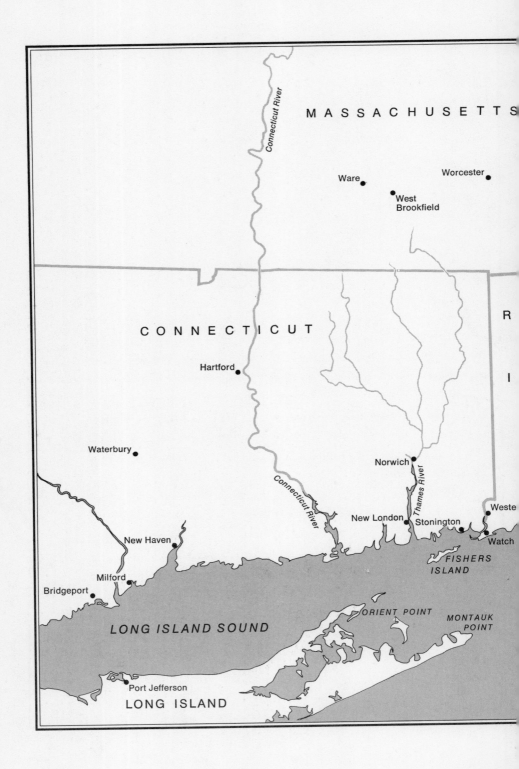

MASSACHUSETTS

Connecticut River

Ware ●

Worcester ●

West Brookfield ●

R

CONNECTICUT

I

Hartford ●

Waterbury ●

Norwich ●

Thames River

Connecticut River

New London ● Stonington ●

Weste ●

Watch ●

FISHERS ISLAND

New Haven ●

Milford ●

Bridgeport ●

ORIENT POINT

MONTAUK POINT

LONG ISLAND SOUND

Port Jefferson ●

LONG ISLAND

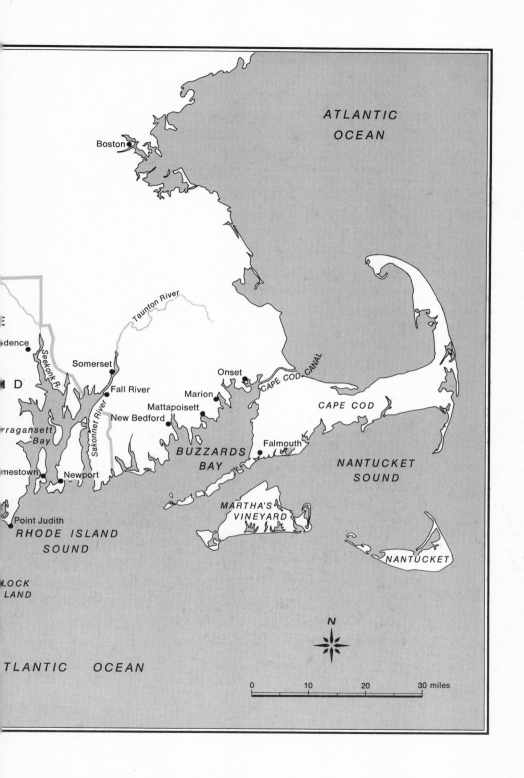

ATLANTIC
OCEAN

Boston

Taunton River

ATLANTIC
OCEAN

dence

Somerset

D   Fall River

Seekonk R.

Onset

Marion

Mattapoisett

New Bedford

CAPE COD CANAL

CAPE COD

Sakonnet River

raganiett
Bay

BUZZARDS
BAY

Falmouth

NANTUCKET
SOUND

mestown   Newport

Point Judith

RHODE ISLAND
SOUND

MARTHA'S
VINEYARD

NANTUCKET

LOCK
LAND

TLANTIC   OCEAN

N

0   10   20   30 miles

favorable; most of the state's shore line is on the protected water of Long Island Sound, where the 120 miles of Long Island stands as a comforting breakwater between the sound and the ocean. The so-called tidal wave, really the hurricane wave driven from the ocean by the southerly gales late in the storm, was able to strike with full flooding force only at the southeast corner of Connecticut, where the coast lies outside Long Island Sound and faces the open sea. It was there that the big waves rushed into the commercial district on New London's waterfront, carrying ships as well as smaller boats over the docks and railroad tracks, and starting a fire that destroyed seventeen buildings. Norwich, an important ocean shipping port in colonial times and now a mill town, stands at the head of the wide Thames River tidal estuary, ten miles upstream from the mouth of the river, where New London is situated. The high wall of ocean waves pushed by the hurricane rolled into the Thames and surged up the river along the course of the annual Harvard-Yale crew races, pouring into the center of Norwich and—in one hour—filling the streets with water eleven feet deep. The crippled and isolated city had to be supplied with food and medicine dropped from planes.

Stonington, a fishing port on the far eastern Connecticut shore near Rhode Island, had in 1938 a fleet of fifty-five fishing boats, most of them owned by fishermen of Portuguese descent. The waterfront extends on a neck of land between Little Narragansett Bay on the east and a small harbor on the west. On the day of the hurricane all the boats were tied up at the docks, some on the east side of the waterfront and the rest of the fleet in the harbor, because the fishermen had been suspicious of the look of the previous evening's sunset. The one-two punch of the hurricane wrecked almost the whole fleet. The gales from the east in the first round of the storm drove green mountains of water across Little Narragansett Bay, smashing the boats on the east docks and wrecking thirty-three houses on that side of the town. After the brief lull, which was hardly noticeable that far from the center of the hurricane, and after the wind switched to the south, the high water from the ocean demolished the docks and boats on the harbor side of the waterfront. Fifty-three of the fifty-five fishing boats were broken, sunk, or thrown ashore. A local resident later said that the fishermen looked at their wrecked boats "as a man might look at his own right hand, cut off at the wrist and thrown on a rubbish heap."

The Shore Line of the New York, New Haven, and Hartford Railroad—its main passenger route from New York to Boston—runs toward Stonington from the west on a long and low causeway with water on both sides of the tracks, the ocean on one side and a tidal estuary on the other. During the hurricane an eastbound express train, the Bostonian, carrying 275 passengers including the group of thirty boys bound for the Fessenden School in Massachusetts, came to a halt on the causeway, with surf breaking against its cars and washing away the rocks under the tracks. On the train was a telephone company repair specialist, Austin S. Burr, who later wrote a report of his experience. While the train was stalled on the causeway, Burr said, he saw a large three-story house being slowly lifted from its foundation. "It floated smoothly before the wind for about fifty yards," he said. "There was a grayishness about everything. The water appeared extremely menacing, not only in its movement but in its color. The surface turned a grayish white, caused by the foam spray, while underneath it was a darker color. As we looked out of the windows, and saw full-sized houses and large boats tossed about by the wind and water, most of us felt complete helplessness."

The engineer, Harry Easton, had stopped the train on the causeway because he had caught sight of a danger signal raised on a signal tower ahead of him. Having climbed down from the cab of the locomotive, Easton waded through water up to his chest to see what the trouble was, and found the track in front of him blocked by a cabin cruiser and an uprooted house. There was also a question of whether the roadbed ahead of the causeway was still strong enough to carry the weight of the entire seven-car train.

Returning to the surf-battered train, Easton learned that its rear cars could not be moved anyway; the tracks were sinking and washing out beneath them, and the waves and debris had broken compressed-air lines, locking their brakes. Trainmen moved the passengers in the rear six cars up to the front car, which was attached to the locomotive. A few panic-stricken people insisted on getting out of the train and trying to walk along the flooded and surf-washed causeway to Stonington. Two of them, a woman passenger and a kitchen worker from the dining car, were swept off the tracks and were drowned.

A trainman, William P. Donoghue, working shoulder-deep in water, succeeded in uncoupling the first car from the rest of the train. Then Easton opened the throttle in the engine and edged gingerly forward, pulling the one crowded passenger car and hoping that the flooded tracks before him would carry its weight and the weight of the locomotive. The engineer carefully pushed the cabin cruiser and then the house off the tracks and chugged on slowly toward higher and drier ground in Stonington. To make the going harder, telegraph wires were hanging low across the tracks and became tangled in the front of the locomotive; Easton found that he was pulling down and dragging telegraph poles as he moved along.

The one-car train pulled into Stonington and stayed there for the night. The women passengers slept in the Catholic church's rectory, and most of the men and the Fessenden School boys (greatly enjoying the excitement), in the Catholic church and the town hall. Since telegraph and telephone lines had been knocked down by the storm, worried railroad executives did not find out where the missing train was until the next day. The news of its escape from the flooded causeway, where the abandoned rear cars were later toppled over by the big surge of hurricane waves, was not reported in the newspapers until two days later.

That night the passengers from the lost train in Stonington saw a red sky in the west over New London, where a fire was burning a quarter-mile area of the waterfront commercial district of the city. The fire had been started during the hurricane, mainly by short-circuited electric wires in the flooded basement of a wholesale grocery company on Banks Street, although it was also reported that storm waves had pushed a big five-masted nautical training ship's bow against a waterfront building, smashing a boiler in the furnace room. Fanned by the hurricane winds, the blaze began to spread from one building to another, as Fire Chief Thomas H. Shipman described it, "as fast as a man could walk." The city's fire alarm system and telephones were knocked out by the storm. Messengers had to be sent on foot to call fire companies, and when fire engines tried to reach the burning buildings, they were blocked by flooded streets, the debris of wrecked houses, and fallen trees. One fire company from the adjoining town of Waterford had to chop its way through thirty trees to get into New London. It seemed for a few hours that the whole city would be burned, but about nine o'clock at night, after seventeen buildings had been destroyed, the firemen managed to halt the spread of the flames with a concentration of twenty streams of water. Then the wind fortunately shifted to the north, from the back of the departed hurricane, containing the fire in the smoldering waterfront area.

At the same time that the fire was being brought under control, the steamboat ferry *Catskill* made its way into the mouth of the Thames estuary in New London after winning a remarkable fight for survival against the hurricane. Its run across the sixteen-mile stretch of water from Orient Point, Long Island, a trip that was usually made in an hour and three quarters, had taken nine hours. The *Catskill* had left Orient Point on its scheduled one thirty departure that afternoon with a light off-season load of three automobiles and eight passengers. When it was almost three quarters of the way across to New London, the captain, a skilled seaman named Sherman, realized that the southeast winds and towering waves pushing him toward Connecticut were so powerful that he would never be able to maneuver the boat into the harbor entrance of the Thames. He turned around, headed back into the gale, and managed miraculously to ride out the hurricane with his ship's engines running. He had plenty of sea room in the comparatively sheltered area of the sound behind the north fork of Long Island. After dark, when the wind subsided, the captain resumed his trip to New London, with his passengers safe and unhurt and his sturdy steamboat undamaged. Having arrived at New London, Sherman found that the ferry dock had been destroyed.

Another Long Island–Connecticut ferryboat, the *Park City*, then running between Port Jefferson and Bridgeport, went through a more terrifying ordeal during the storm. The *Park City*, a 150-foot steamer with nine crew members, five adult passengers, and a two-month-old baby aboard, was adrift without engine power and with no radio contact for twenty-one hours. The ferryboat had left Port Jefferson on its scheduled trip to Bridgeport at two o'clock on the afternoon of the hurricane. The weather then, with a brisk southeast wind, did not seem to be particularly dangerous. When the steamboat was well into the middle of Long Island Sound, about five miles from Port Jefferson, the wind and the waves suddenly became so overpowering that the captain, Ray Dickerson, tried to turn the steamer back toward Long Island. Unable to make any progress against the gale and boiling waves, he dropped the anchor but it dragged. Waves washed across the decks of the boat and water rushed into the hold, putting out the fires in the boilers and flooding the generator, thereby extinguishing electric power and lights. As the boat rolled and bobbed helplessly in the waves, the passengers and crew could only pray. All of them remained calm during the storm and in the long hours of complete darkness that followed it, Captain Dickerson said later. Even the baby did not cry.

At 7:15 the next morning the drifting ferryboat was sighted by a Coast Guard cutter that had come from Staten Island to patrol Long Island Sound. It took the cutter's crew an hour to get a tow line on the steamboat, and three more hours to tow it into Port Jefferson. After landing back at the same dock where they had started their trip the previous day, the passengers hurried away without a word of complaint, glad to be alive. One of them, a mysterious young woman, firmly refused to tell her name or address, or to say where she had been going when her journey was interrupted by the hurricane.

Although Connecticut's Long Island Sound shore line was more sheltered from hurricane surf than the coasts of Long Island, Rhode Island, and Buzzards Bay in Massachusetts, there was widespread damage from high tides and wind along the beaches and harbors from Greenwich to New London. One family from Darien happened to be sailing in their schooner on the sound when the storm struck; they rode out the hurricane safely on the rough water, but when they returned to their home on the shore that night, they found their house ruined. Among the hurricane refugees on the Connecticut shore was Katharine Hepburn, who waded to safety through the flooding tide from her parents' summer cottage at Fenwick, near the mouth of the Connecticut River, an hour before the cottage was carried away.

The Connecticut tobacco crop was ruined by the hurricane, at a loss of several million dollars. Most of the broadleaf tobacco grown along the Connecticut River valley as wrappers for cigars had been picked and was drying in sheds heated by charcoal braziers. The gales blew down the sheds, and many of them caught fire from the braziers and burned. The greatest destruction in the state was caused by floods that rushed downstream in the rivers of Connecticut, especially the Connecticut River, after the downpour of the hurricane's torrential rains had soaked the hills and valleys of northern New England.

On the day after the storm, the Connecticut River, which had been swollen even before the hurricane, was up to thirty-three feet above its low-water level at Hartford and still rising. An emergency dike of sandbags had been hurriedly built along Sheldon Street beside the reinforced Colt Dike, near the Colt firearms factory, but Army engineers gave the barrier only a 50-50 chance of holding the river back from the city. If the dike had broken, Hartford would have suffered a major disaster. The Colt factory buildings would have been destroyed, and several big old storage tanks would probably have been uprooted and hurled against the Hartford Electric Light Company generating plant. While an army of two thousand WPA workers, city employees, and thirteen hundred volunteers worked frantically to keep the top of the mile-long barrier of sandbags above the rising water, city officials made plans to dynamite an outlet for the flood farther south on the river below the city.

At ten o'clock on Friday night, however, the river reached a peak of 35.1 feet and stopped its rise without breaking through the dike; cheers of triumph resounded along the muddy wall of sandbags. "Churches fairly hummed with prayers of thanksgiving," an excited Hartford *Courant* reporter wrote. It was later discovered that five hundred of the thirteen hundred volunteer workers hired for the emergency by the WPA, most of them college students, never collected their pay.

*　*　*　*

When the first gales of the hurricane struck the Rhode Island coast, four tourists—three young men and a girl—were sight-seeing on the beach of Napatree Point at Watch Hill, which was to become a few hours later the scene of one of the storm's greatest tragedies. Napatree Point, the most western point of land on the Rhode Island shore, is a narrow sandspit extending for more than a mile between the ocean and Little Narragansett Bay, the wide body of water that lies between the attractive residential summer resort on the steep high ground at Watch Hill and the distant shore near Stonington, Connecticut. As its name suggests, Napatree Point was once covered with trees and grass, but all its timber and vegetation had been washed away in the big New England hurricane of 1815, leaving only the bare strip of sand that now serves as the Watch Hill colony's ocean bathing beach.

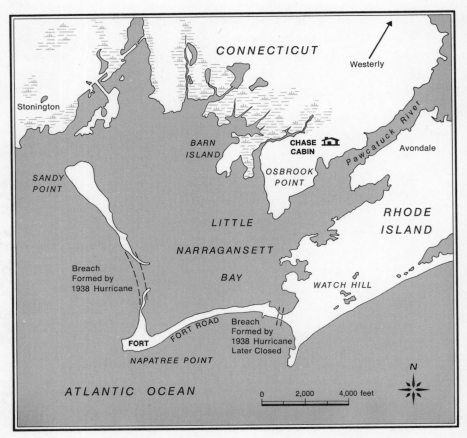

In 1938 before the hurricane there was a beach club building and a pavilion of bathhouses on the ocean side of Napatree
Point, near the small center of shops and stores at the foot of
Watch Hill; on the bay side were the local yacht club and its
dock. Beyond the beach club and the yacht club, along the Fort
Road, which then ran along Napatree Point to the old abandoned coast artillery post of Fort Mansfield at its far end, there
were thirty-nine cottages occupied by summer residents. During
the height of the hurricane, according to a later count, there

were forty-two people in the cottages on the Fort Road despite the lateness of the summer vacation season. Some of the families remained in their oceanfront cottages that late in September because the husbands and smaller children could drive to business and to schools in the nearby city of Westerly, Rhode Island, where they lived in the winter; their older sons and daughters did not have to leave for college until later in the week.

The only people who remained alive on Napatree Point throughout the hurricane were the four tourists. They were saved because they happened to be looking at the ramparts at Fort Mansfield, at the far end of the beach, when the storm struck, and they took shelter in one of its concrete gun emplacement pits. The pit was flooded when the big surge of storm waves washed over it, but the three men managed to tread water, holding up the hysterical girl between them. The old fort was the only structure on Napatree Point that was still there after the storm. All the other buildings on the beach—the beach club and pavilion, the yacht club, and every one of the cottages on the Fort Road—were swept into Little Narragansett Bay. Some of the structures were broken up and washed away in the surf that rolled from the ocean to the bay before the climax of the storm. The rest were demolished by the massive surge of waves that came towering over the beach after the wind shifted from the east to the south. A man who was securing a yacht to the sea wall on Watch Hill's bayside waterfront when the big hurricane surge rushed in from the ocean said later that he saw it "covering everything on the Fort Road like a long roll of cotton," while the yacht club was splitting into two pieces, with a piano sailing out of its broken roof and "flying twenty feet in the air like a big bird." All forty-two people who were in the cottages on the Fort Road were swept into the bay. Fifteen of them were

69

drowned. The others, clinging to pieces of wreckage, were carried by the hurricane gales for more than two miles across the bay to its Connecticut shore, where most of them were washed up around Osbrook Point, near the Pawcatuck River.

That night, after the tide and the winds had subsided, the three men and the girl at the old fort made their way back along Napatree Point toward Watch Hill, a walk that must have seemed like a nightmare to them. The cottages that they had passed earlier in the day had disappeared and the beach was empty, except for a few twisted telephone poles. They found themselves cut off from the mainland by a new inlet dug through the beach from the ocean to the bay by the hurricane. The men shouted for help, and the group was finally rescued by a local fisherman who had to make four trips through the swift current of the inlet because his small rowboat could hold only one passenger at a time.

After the storm Charles F. Hammond, who was then the publisher of Watch Hill's summer weekly newspaper, *Seaside Topics*, decided to put out a special hurricane issue of his paper, devoted to pictures of the widespread local damage and to stories of the Napatree Point disaster. Hammond succeeded in persuading several women who had survived the terror of the hurricane on the Fort Road to write about the experience while it was still fresh in their minds. He was also able to obtain for publication in *Seaside Topics* a long and fully detailed letter that Mrs. Geoffrey Moore, another Napatree Point survivor, had written to her brother about her family's escape from the hurricane. These firsthand reports, put down on paper by the survivors themselves, give a clear picture of courage in the face of death. As Hammond wrote in the introduction to his hurricane documentary, which has since been republished by *Seaside*

Topics in pamphlet form, "Out of the stories of the survivors, there comes a new confidence in the fortitude of the human spirit."

Along with the letter of Mrs. Geoffrey Moore, who stood beside her husband, who had just suffered a heart attack, and her four young children, who were quietly praying, as she awaited the destruction of her wave-smashed cottage, Hammond included the story of her sister-in-law, Mrs. Cyril V. Moore, who made her way across the bay with her uncomplaining six-year-old daughter in her arms. There are also the cool recollections of Helen Joy Lee, firmly self-possessed even though she was entirely alone during the hurricane and for twelve more hours after she landed on the Connecticut shore; and the story of the frail and elderly Jane Grey Stevenson, the gentle proprietress of a Watch Hill gift shop, who climbed out of the surging water in the bay and clung to a broken roof after her sister and her maid had been drowned beside her. "Wreckage was all around me and the waves were very high," Miss Stevenson wrote in *Seaside Topics*, "but one thing made me laugh, even in the midst of that horror—I saw a can of coffee from my kitchen shelf bobbing along beside me, as though to make sure I would have coffee at my destination."

Nobody at Watch Hill, or anywhere else in Rhode Island, had heard any warning of a hurricane or of the possibility of any kind of extremely dangerous storm that Wednesday. The big waves came upon Napatree Point so suddenly and unexpectedly that only five of the people who were there at that time were able to escape by automobile before several of the cottages on the road began to wash away, about three thirty in the afternoon. Water was then flooding the dining room of Geoffrey Moore's big house on Fort Road, a sturdy three-story dwelling that was the last one on the point to be destroyed in the hurricane. Jeff Moore's wife, Catherine, suggested that they ought to make a run for their winter home in Westerly, where Jeff and his three brothers managed a family textile mill. It would be a rough drive, they knew. Andy Pupillo, their young handy man, said that he had almost been blown off the road several times while driving two of the children home from school a short time earlier. There were ten people in the house when the storm struck; besides Jeff and Catherine and their four children— Geoffrey, Jr., twelve, Anne, ten, Cathy, eight, and Margaret, who was then four years old—and a visiting relative, May Doherty, the Moores had three servants: Andy, a maid named Loretta, and Nancy, the cook. When Catherine suggested leaving the beach house because "it looked very serious to me," her husband said that she and the women and girls could go to Westerly with Andy as their driver, but that he and young Geoffrey would stay behind to look after the place. "I refused to go unless everyone went," Mrs. Moore wrote later to her brother, so everybody stayed.

Even before the hurricane, Mrs. Moore said in her letter to her brother, it had been a day when everything seemed to go wrong. In the morning, Anne's sailboat had broken loose from its mooring, and Andy and Geoffrey had been blown across the bay in a rowboat trying to recover it. (Mrs. Moore called her son Geoffrey to distinguish him from Jeff, her husband.) Jeff had had to be summoned from his office at the mill to rescue the two boys, and after the exertion and a hasty lunch, he had suffered a mild heart attack. The doctor called to examine him had ordered Jeff to remain in bed for the next three days. Two hours later, when waves from the ocean were breaking against the second-floor windows, and the window in the living room downstairs had crashed in, Jeff was out of bed and trying to nail winter shutters against the windows. "He called for something bigger, a door," Mrs. Moore wrote. "I went down cellar and brought one up, the water nearly to my knees." Mrs. Moore, a small woman, probably never would have tried to carry a heavy door upstairs from the cellar alone at any other time. (After the hurricane people were amazed when they recalled the feats of strength that they had been able to perform under stress during the storm.)

Then the Moores realized that they had a newly arrived refugee in their house, Jim Nestor, an eighteen-year-old boy from Providence who had been visiting his aunt, Anne Nestor, at the cottage next door. The cottage had been washed away but Jim had managed to escape from it. Jeff Moore asked him what had happened to his aunt and the two maids who had been working at the cottage. "They are gone," Jim said.

"And then the horror of the whole thing gripped me," Mrs. Moore wrote in her letter. "I felt we had small hope of our lives. Jeff told everybody to stay together no matter what happened. We decided to stand on the second floor between the Green Room and the hall, hoping that the doorcasing would help in case the house crashed in on us. May prayed aloud in a firm and confident voice as she clutched a picture of Christ. Cathy came to me and said, 'Mummy, if I *must* die, I want my rosary.' I went to my room and found a little blue rosary and told her to put it over her head. It wouldn't fit so I wound it around her wrist.

"There were no more outcries from Cathy, she was quiet and just waited. With Cathy quiet, Margaret with her hand in mine said nothing. As we stood there, waiting, Loretta asked me if I didn't want my pocketbook, but I told her it didn't matter, material things just didn't count any more. I told every-

73

body to take off his shoes in case we had to swim.

"Jeff said good-bye to me, but I told him not to give up yet. I asked him to watch out for Cathy, Jim to watch out for May, and Andy to take care of Loretta and Nancy. I said I would take Margaret. Geoffrey and Anne I knew could take care of themselves better than any of us. I had previously put coats and life-savers on Margaret and Cathy and one on May. I could only find three. I asked Geoffrey to put a sweater on, as he had no shirt on but he didn't. I told everyone, but particularly the girls, to grab onto some large floating object if they found themselves in the water. There was no panic. We all prayed constantly, sometimes silently and sometimes aloud. Suddenly the house began to collapse beneath us. We ran, with lightning speed and as a unit, down the hall and up the stairs to the third floor, and just in time, for the second floor had gone down like an elevator only with a sideways motion. The sea wall and the foundation were being hurled about below us. I watched some nice new pink curtains wash out of the linen closet but the main thing I saw was a raging ocean where the girls' room had been at the foot of the stairs."

The Moores surveyed their situation under the sloping roof of the small third-floor area, where there was a maid's room, the cook's room, and a bathroom, and felt that they would be trapped between the floor and the roof if the top part of the house was washed or blown away. Jeff broke the glass in the bathroom window so that they would have an opening to escape through, and a torrent of water came into the bathroom from the jagged hole. The children prayed.

"I heard Anne say, 'Now say it, Margaret, say it after me,'" Mrs. Moore wrote. "'Oh, my God, I am heartily sorry . . .' 'Oh,

74

my God, I am heartily sorry . . .' 'For having offended Thee . . .'
'For having offended Thee . . .' and right through the Act of
Contrition. All these little things inspired us to keep up our
courage—these little ones facing death so gallantly and in the
proper manner."

Then the roof blew off the maid's room, making its exposed floor an ideal raft, with two broken pipes sticking up
through the floor to serve as supports to hang on to. The group
of eleven people huddled together in sitting positions on the
floor, Mrs. Moore grasping one of the pipes and holding Cathy
with her other arm, and Jeff, with Margaret in his arms, bend-
ing one of his legs around the other pipe. May held one of
Jeff's arms and Anne held him from the back. The others clung
together closely around the parents and the smaller children.
The big waves washed over them and carried them on the raftlike floor into the bay, where the surf was so high that they
thought for a while that they had been swept across the other
side of the beach into the ocean. The spray from the surf, and
the mist and rain, were so thick that they could not see where
they were heading. The wall between the maid's room and the
cook's room next to it had remained vertically attached to the
floor platform and served as a sail, pushing them along swiftly
in the hurricane gales. Then Jeff announced that he could see
a few of the telephone poles on Fort Road behind them, which
was good news because it meant that they were in the bay and
not adrift in the ocean. A few minutes later, as the waves around
them became smaller, they sighted the Dennison Rock buoy,
which is more than halfway across the bay toward the Connecticut shore.

"About this time we heard our parrot, which Loretta had

let out of her cage, say from somewhere, 'Hello, Polly,' " Mrs. Moore wrote. "We prayed harder that we would make the other side. Pretty soon I saw land in the hazy distance."

*   *   *   *

Unlike the Geoffrey Moore family and most of the other survivors of the Napatree Point disaster, Helen Joy Lee was alone all during the hurricane and through the night that followed it after she came ashore on Osbrook Point. Mrs. Lee, daughter of Henry B. Joy, the founder of the Packard Motor Car Company, has been a lifelong summer resident of Watch Hill. In 1938 she was occupying the fourth cottage from the far end of Fort Road on Napatree Point, out near the old abandoned artillery ramparts of Fort Mansfield, about a mile from the shopping center of Watch Hill. Mrs. Lee's two daughters, Marian and Eunice, were spending the summer with her. In the morning of the day of the hurricane, Marian had borrowed her mother's car and gone off for the rest of the day. The weather at noon was not bad enough to stop Mrs. Lee and Eunice from taking their usual before-lunch swim in the ocean, although they did not venture out beyond the breaking waves. After their swim they bathed their dog, and Eunice went off to have lunch with friends and go to the movies, leaving Mrs. Lee alone in the beach cottage with the dog and a small kitten.

"About three, I thought I would walk to the village, but the wind was blowing the sand on the road and it stung my legs, so I stayed home," Mrs. Lee wrote in her account of the storm for *Seaside Topics*. "The wind shifted more to the east. Then to the northeast and stronger. About three thirty the wind veered to the south. For some ten minutes, the ocean had no whitecaps but looked as though a spoon was stirring white milk into a green cake mixture. Then the wind came up and the surf started pounding."

Mrs. Lee was one of the few survivors on Napatree Point to notice the eerie lull before the worst blow of the storm; others remembered only a barely perceptible shift in the wind. Having seen two cyclonic storms in Florida, Mrs. Lee realized from watching the renewal of strong gales and high surf after the lull that this storm was probably a tropical hurricane. If it was a hurricane, she reminded herself reassuringly from her Florida experience, the wind would be violent for a short period but it would soon decrease.

Mrs. Lee put on a raincoat, tucked her small kitten into a pocket of the coat, tied her German shepherd to the inside knob of the back door, and went out the door onto the back porch to have a look around. While she was on the porch, a gust of wind broke the front door of the cottage and rushed inside, slamming the back door shut on the porch behind her and breaking the glass panel. The wind picked the kitten out of her coat pocket and it sailed away in the air. Getting back into the house was impossible; it was so filled with wind and water that she could not push open the back door. Mrs. Lee reached through the empty space in the door where the glass had shattered and lifted the dog outside to the porch. Then she sat with the dog on a pile of firewood logs to wait for whatever would happen next.

During the storm and after it, Mrs. Lee was wearing a waterproof wrist watch, which enabled her to keep an accurate check on the time. "At four thirty I was sitting on the wood-pile on the porch with the dog, saying aloud, 'I wonder how much longer,'" she wrote in *Seaside Topics*. "Something hit the front of the house, I think it might have been a section of the retaining wall, and a wave washed into my lap. It knocked the porch down, something broke my left arm, and the dog and I were washed into the bay, as if on a roller coaster, all in ten seconds. I looked up and saw the lattice of the porch coming at me. I ducked under some squares of our sidewalk, which I had seen washed out like stamps, and the lattice went over my head. I reached the dog and undid the leash and she floated off on a door, and so on to dog heaven. The kitten, which had left my pocket twenty minutes earlier, was floating on a board ten feet from me."

Mrs. Lee clung to a pole in the water with her uninjured arm, tried to climb aboard a section of roof that capsized, and then clung to a smaller piece of house siding.

"I was hit on the head many times by wood," she wrote, "one piece like a bookcase gave me a black eye. A splinter of wood was taken out of the bridge of my nose later and my head had many cuts and bruises. When I was in the trough of a wave I could look. up and see shutters, chairs, and pillows getting blown off the wave tops, so when I was coming up the side of the wave I tried to ward things off with my one arm. The roof top returned, V up, so I crawled into it, as it was solid at one end toward the wind, and gave protection.

"I rode this quite a while, often having to hold my hand over nose and mouth to be able to breathe. Then a mattress came, and was moving faster, so I got on that. It was getting gray, the wind seemed not so strong, and I dimly saw some tree-tops. A boat with two feet remaining on the port bow and about five feet on the starboard came by and as that gave more cover I again transferred. The boat went *over* some trees. I could just see the tips out of the water. Another ten minutes and it was dark and the boat stuck. I crawled out and found land, but water also up to my armpits. I pushed through the debris and got to a tree. I sat on a limb just at the water level and hung there."

Mrs. Lee's watch told her that it was six thirty when she landed on the Connecticut shore and climbed onto the tree branch, which meant that she had been floating in Little Narragansett Bay for two hours. Another hour and a half passed before the water around the tree dropped down to the level of her hanging feet, allowing her finally to leave her seat on the limb. The rain had stopped. She found herself standing in a foot of water and she thought that she was enveloped in a thick fog; later, when she saw stars in the sky she realized that her eyes were fogged with film. She picked up two shingles, sat on one of them in water up to her waist at the foot of the tree, and placed the other shingle between the base of her spine and the lower trunk of the tree, so that she could lean back against it. She sat in this position for the next twelve hours during the long night, from eight in the evening until four the next morning. "I pulled my arms inside my sweater and put my head on my knees," she wrote. "I made myself get up and stretch several times, and called out to keep warm."

At four in the morning, when her eyes had cleared and she could see better, Mrs. Lee began to walk across the surrounding swamps, falling three times into ditches. As it was getting light, she found a road and followed it to a house where smoke was coming out of a chimney.

"Not wanting to scare the people, as I knew I looked wild, I called out," she wrote. "A man came out, just stared at me, then asked where I came from. I said I had been washed from Fort Road. I went in the house, sat by the stove, and shook from nerves, not cold, for an hour. A cup of coffee, a wait of another hour or so—it was 6:25 when I got there—another half-mile walk to a car, and Mr. Fred Greenwood and another man took me to the hospital. My children did not know my fate until nine Thursday morning when Dr. Kenyon at the Westerly Hospital offered to go and tell them I had turned up, alive."

*   *   *   *

Jane Stevenson managed a gift shop in the old schoolhouse building at Watch Hill for many years before and after the hurricane. In the winter months, when her shop was closed, she traveled in Europe buying merchandise for it. In September of 1938 she was living with her sister Mary, who was ill with diabetes, and their maid, Elliefair Price, at an oceanfront cottage on Fort Road, which she called Stevecot. Talking recently about Jane Stevenson, who died not long ago, a friend of hers in Watch Hill said, "If you read Jane's story in *Seaside Topics*, about her survival in the hurricane, without knowing anything about her, you might assume that she was a young and rugged woman at the time of the storm. Actually, I'd say that she was then in her late sixties, probably around sixty-seven or sixty-eight, and she was a little bit of a thing, fragile-looking and shy and timid. You'd think that she would faint in fright at the very mention of a hurricane, and I could never picture her struggling in the bay that day, hanging on to the shingles on a wrecked roof. It shows you what people can do when they have to do it to live. Jane did have one favorite habit, though, that probably was the thing that saved her in the hurricane—every day she took a swim in the ocean from

80

Wrecked automobiles and other debris littered the beach at Westhampton, Long Island (right), after the hurricane of 1938.

An aerial view of Fire Island
shows an inlet to Great South
Bay created by the hurricane.

A row of summer houses had stood on the beach at Westhampton (above).

A storm-tossed boat was found near a wrecked train in Connecticut.

Piers and boats at New London, Connecticut (above), were ripped apart by the hurricane; storm damage in New London was estimated at $4,000,000. At right is a view of flood-inundated Weybosset Street in downtown Providence. Below, workmen at Hartford erect levees to control the rapidly rising Connecticut River.

The Mall, Providence, Rhode Island, on September 21, 1938

PROVIDENCE *Journal-Bulletin*

The turreted section of this home seems to defy gravity.

A derailed train plowed into a house in Highland Falls, New York.

UNITED PRESS INTERNATIONAL

UNITED PRESS INTERNATIONAL

A Rhode Island home was washed off its foundations by the floods.

This home in Misquamicut had been called Pleasant View.

NEW YORK *Daily News*

In Onset, Massachusetts, many houses were blown off their foundations.

Storm wreckage filled the streets of South Dartmouth in Massachusetts.

the beach in front of her cottage on Fort Road, so she certainly wasn't afraid of water."

On the afternoon of the hurricane, Jane closed her shop early, after three o'clock, and went to her cottage on the point to be with her ailing sister, "who had been ill all summer and was easily frightened." Jane noted in her story in *Seaside Topics* that "like everyone else, I thought that this was just an unusually high wind which would subside toward evening." A high dune on the ocean side of her cottage blocked her view of the sea, so while she and her sister were having tea at four o'clock, she noticed only that the waves sounded louder than usual. When the windows of the cottage began to blow in and water ran through the rooms, Jane remained calm because she was certain that the Coast Guard would evacuate the people on Napatree Point if the storm became dangerous. "My sister and our little maid and I went into the kitchen on the bay side of the house," she wrote, "to be ready when the Coast Guard should come for us. I even packed a bag with things we would need overnight. I had felt so sure that they would come, as in times past they had brought boats when there was high water on the Fort Road, and because of that hope I had not the slightest fear. I was standing in water up to my knees, the other two sitting on a table to keep dry, when the chimney fell into the room, the walls began to sway, cans and dishes fell from the shelves, and suddenly the little house simply fell to pieces and we were shot into the water."

Apparently Mary Stevenson and Miss Price, the maid, were both drowned immediately—their bodies were found later—because Jane could not see them anywhere around her when she came to the surface in the bay.

"In fact, I could not see more than a few feet in any direction on account of the heavy mist, like a thick fog," she wrote, "but close to me was a piece of roof onto which I climbed, kneeling and holding the shingles to keep steady. I saw no other person all the time I was in the water, and had no idea where I was. It seemed a good part of the time as though I were going around in circles. Wreckage was all around me and the waves were very high. After floating a long time, sliding off several times and climbing up again, seeing and hearing nobody—though I kept on calling—the mist seemed to clear and I saw trees, and saw that wreckage was piling up in one place so I knew there was land near and shouted with all my strength. A welcome voice answered and I saw someone near me."

The other refugee, who landed near Miss Stevenson, was Mrs. John C. Warner, a neighbor from Fort Road who had floated across the bay on a door after her house had been demolished. The cry that Miss Stevenson had shouted "with all [her] strength" sounded so faint to Mrs. Warner that it could barely be heard. Mrs. Warner urged Miss Stevenson to climb over the wreckage and helped her to walk from the shore at Osbrook Point across a flooded cornfield to a road. There the two wet and exhausted women met Herbert Greenman, a carpenter who had been closing a cottage on Fort Road for the winter when the big waves came. Greenman and his helper, Frank Pasetti, had been thrown into the bay, where Pasetti had drowned. Greenman, with broken ribs, was about to give up trying to swim when he saw a rag doll floating by him in a bathtub, its legs rising and falling in the bobbing of the waves. He laughed and shouted at the doll, "Old girl, if you can make it, I can!" Resuming his struggle for survival, he finally reached the shore at Osbrook Point, where he walked with Miss Stevenson and Mrs. Warner until they discovered the small cabin where George Chase, a caretaker for the surrounding property, made his home. Chase's cabin was only large enough to hold his one bed, a few chairs, and his wood-burning stove, but it served that night as a warm refuge for several people from Napatree Point, who gratefully drank hot ginger tea served to them by their host as a remedy for cold and exposure.

Chase's ginger tea, Jane Stevenson recalled later, "burned all the way down, but made me feel warm and alive. Then he gave me his overcoat and made me take off all my wet clothes, which he hung on a line over the stove. No praise can be too great for Mr. Chase's warm sympathy to all of us in that little house." In the morning, after she had been taken to Westerly, Jane learned that her sister's body had been found on Osbrook Point near where she and Mrs. Warner had landed. Mary's body was so unrecognizable that it was identified only by a white cotton sock that she had been wearing on one foot to protect an infection.

*   *   *   *

The rag doll that had encouraged Herbert Greenman to keep on swimming in the bay belonged to six-year-old Mary Moore, daughter of Cyril Moore, Jeff's brother, who was at work at his family's mill in Westerly when his cottage on the Fort Road was demolished in the hurricane. Mary and her mother, Harriet Moore, who was with her in the beach cottage during the storm, also ended up spending the night in George Chase's cabin, along with Margaret Kane, their maid, and two friends, Mrs. Arthur M. Cottrell, Jr., and Denise O'Brien, who had been visiting them at Napatree Point that afternoon.

95

"Mary Moore is one of the bravest children I have ever known," Mrs. Cottrell wrote after the storm. When the rag doll was found the next day, Mary presented it to Greenman as a remembrance of his survival in the hurricane and he kept it forever afterward, calling it affectionately Hurricane Sue.

On her way home from school on the day of the storm, Mary got off the school bus at the Watch Hill Golf Club to meet her mother, who had been playing golf there with Mrs. Cottrell and Miss O'Brien. While the three women were waiting for Mary's arrival on the bus, all the awnings blew off the clubhouse. Mrs. Moore telephoned her maid, Margaret, at her beach home to make sure that all was well there. Having been assured by Margaret that the cottage did not seem to be in any danger, Mrs. Moore invited Mrs. Cottrell and Miss O'Brien to follow her and Mary home to the beach in their cars so that they could spend the rest of the afternoon there watching the spectacle of the surf.

They reached the beach house about 3:45, just when the wind had shifted to the south and the huge storm waves were beginning to roar over the dunes from the ocean. While the women were standing at the dining room window watching the suddenly rising surf, the wind smashed the glass out of the porch windows on the west side of the house and swept the furniture off the porch, including a metal hammock, which was thrown fifty yards into a picture window of the cottage next door. The waves began to wash across the porch, gradually flooding the living room next to it. Mrs. Moore and her friends decided to move the furniture in the living room away from the water and took down the new curtains, which had just been put up. Taking down the living room curtains and carefully folding them and placing them in a chest in the dining room to keep them dry when the whole house was about to be washed away seemed later to Denise O'Brien to be "perhaps the most ludicrous thing we did." "We had no sooner finished this task than the ocean moved into the living room," Miss O'Brien wrote later. "Another humorous touch was going upstairs for a raincoat for Mary Moore. The waves thought so, too, as they peeped into the bedroom window to see what we were up to."

When the waves began to break against the roof of the house, which had been built high, with two floors above the top of the dunes, the women decided that they would be less likely to get wet in the garage downstairs. "I was so confident about the construction of the house that I knew nothing would happen to us," Harriet Moore wrote later in her account of the storm in *Seaside Topics*. "All the time we had been perfectly calm. I was the last person to go down to the garage with the dogs. I stopped on the way to put five letters which I had written that morning where they would be safe, put my watch in the kitchen cupboard, and took two coats of Cy's with me so that he would have something dry to put on that night when he came home. I put the dogs in the station wagon where they would be safe and dry and we stood around quite casually and certainly not upset."

Then the southwest corner of the house was torn away from the rest of the structure, carrying a coal stove with it, and the women in the garage found themselves up to their necks in water. On the outside of the house there was a flight of stairs leading up to the kitchen door on the floor above the garage. The outside staircase was protected by latticework that enclosed it completely, and there was a lattice door leading into the enclosed stairs. Mrs. Moore picked up Mary and she and the other women made their way from the flooded garage around the outside back corner of the house to the outside stairs, hoping to get up to the kitchen and then to go up to the attic to escape the deluge. They had a hard time trying to open the lattice door at the foot of the staircase, and then, when they reached the top of the stairs, they found that the door leading into the kitchen was locked and could not be broken open.

Going back down the stairs seemed dangerous, so they stayed at the top of the stairs outside the locked kitchen door, with the gale winds and the surf blowing through the lattice-work enclosure around them. A few minutes earlier Mrs. Moore had been amazed to see that the Watts cottage next door had been carried intact from its foundations into the bay. Then she realized that she could see no houses at all along the beach to the east or to the west of her. The women tried desperately to kick in the door but could not budge it, and Mrs. Moore went down to the foot of the steps and picked up a heavy piece of wood to use against it. As she climbed back up to the small landing at the top of the stairs in front of the door, a platform three feet square, Violet Cottrell and Denise O'Brien moved a few steps down the stairs to give her room to work on the door. Then a huge wave carried away the staircase with Mrs. Cottrell and Miss O'Brien on it, breaking it off from the top landing at the door to the kitchen where Mrs. Moore, Mary, and Margaret Kane, the maid, were left stranded on the three-foot-square platform.

"The last I saw of Vio and Denise was the soles of their shoes being carried along as the house seemed to settle," Mrs. Moore wrote later. "Margaret looked at me and I looked at her. Not a word was said. With the recession of that wave, the house seemed to rise again. Another wave hit us which did no great damage; a second wave after that hit us and took down the plastering along this enclosed stairway, and I can remember trying to pull away the plaster to make a hole so we could escape from the enclosure, but the plaster lathings were so close together that I could not get my fingers in between them.

"It was a desperate moment. A third wave came and Margaret said, 'Gracious, there goes the kitchen stove!' and I said, 'Yes, and the icebox, too.' The fourth wave came and I felt the house give. The ceiling over our heads opened up and I said to Mary and Margaret, 'We will all hold hands and lean on the kitchen door.' The next thing I knew we were out in the bay, Mary in my arms and Margaret and I clutching each other. I was able to get my feet on the ground for a moment, which was a great help. Margaret reached out for a piece of roofing which was floating by and we were able to get ourselves up on it. It was about the size of a bed. We found it very difficult to stay on as the shingles kept coming off. We shared the responsibility of holding Mary, as she was on my back and then on Margaret's but all the time between us. I can remember the child saying many times, 'Margaret, Mummy says it's all right.' "

Meanwhile, Mrs. Cottrell and Miss O'Brien, whom Mrs. Moore assumed to be drowned, had seen the house from the bay as it cracked open and fell into the water. They were clutching a mattress that had floated between them and were debating, in screams to make themselves heard above the roar of the wind, whether they ought to go back and help the others; but trying to go back against the surf was impossible.

"There was an appalling cracking noise, the most horrifying I have ever heard," Mrs. Cottrell wrote in her account of the storm. "The house split squarely down the middle, toppled, and thundered into the water. It was so awful I think it stunned us. I remember saying, 'God, forgive us!' and asking Miss O'Brien whether she thought we could have reached the Moores in time. We never thought we would see them alive again."

As Mrs. Moore and Margaret Kane—stretched out flat on their stomachs on the slab of roofing—made their way across the bay in the high waves with six-year-old Mary between them, their biggest worry was trying to keep debris from piling up on their backs. They were nearing shore at Osbrook Point when a wave broke their raft into two pieces, washing Margaret, the maid, away to the right and dumping Mrs. Moore, with Mary in her arms, into the water, which was shallow enough for her to walk in through the debris and surf.

"We managed to struggle to dry land," Mrs. Moore wrote. "Margaret in the meantime had been washed ashore and she said it seemed like a year until we were finally together again. It was dark. My only idea was to keep going inland with the wind at our backs and I am afraid I was very stern with Mary about not stopping anywhere. We held Mary's hands and started to run. The poor child, utterly exhausted, dropped and said, 'Mummy, I just can't.' I really thought we had lost her. She fell on her face and when I turned her over foam was coming out of her mouth, so I beat her with my fists on the back which was apparently the right thing to do for she came to immediately and we decided that the foam was the salt water she had swallowed. We were lost most desperately in the thick brambles and underbrush and we had a terrible time trying to get over fallen trees. A herd of sheep flew by us and scared us almost to death, but we were very much cheered because I knew that if there were sheep there must be people in the neighborhood.

"We were getting nowhere and it was still raining and I

knew we were all pretty well exhausted but must keep on. We passed one little shack. I was most profuse in saying there were no signs of habitation and we just seemed to have to get on, as I knew in our wet clothes and in our exhausted condition, it was no place for us to spend the night. We passed two stone wall fences, passed another shack, and about three hundred yards after we passed the last shack, who should be coming down the road toward us but Vio, Denise, and a man. That meeting was more than words can say, because each of us thought we would never see the other again."

The reunited friends and the man, Joe Reardon, a carpenter who had been working on a house at Napatree Point when the hurricane struck, went to George Chase's cabin, where they found Jane Stevenson, Mrs. Warner, Herbert Greenman, and two other carpenters, Ed Fiddes and Jerry Shea, who had been trapped on the beach with Reardon. The little cabin was so cramped with this influx of refugees that as Mrs. Moore noted, "it was necessary to do no moving when we were once seated—three on the bed, two on the floor, two on the wood box, three on backless stools, and Mary on one of the carpenters' laps, just like peas in a pod."

By nine o'clock that night the sky was clear with the stars shining, and the air was cold with little wind. There was nothing to eat in the cabin and only a bottle of milk and a pail of stale water to drink. Jerry Shea, nervous about his family, decided to walk to Westerly and persuaded George Chase to show him the way as far as the nearby farm of the Davis family. Shea wrote down on a piece of paper the names of everyone in the cabin. When he reached Westerly, he gave the paper to a small boy and asked the boy to deliver it to the Red Cross emergency relief headquarters in the town. The Red Cross contacted Max

Cottrell, Violet's husband, and also sent a group of six men headed by Arthur Dionne to the cabin on foot. Miss O'Brien and Mrs. Cottrell, worried about her husband, who had been ill before the storm, decided to walk to Westerly with the men in Dionne's group, but Mrs. Moore, not wanting to put little Mary through such a march in the darkness, decided to stay in the cabin until morning with Miss Stevenson, Mrs. Warner, and Margaret Kane. After the others had left, making more room in the small cabin for those who remained, Mary and Margaret managed to sleep, covered with newspapers, on the floor. "Once Mary stood up, looked at me and said, 'Mummy, you look tired,'" Mrs. Moore wrote. "All this time she had been absolutely perfect—not once did she cry, whimper, or say 'I am scared' or 'Don't leave me, Mummy.' She did what she was told and was in every way marvelous beyond words. A great tribute to me. Margaret, too, had played her part like a Trojan. By this time, my legs had begun to swell, my ankles as big as my knees, and I apparently had a bad gash on my knee for I found myself covered with blood."

Another searching party, headed by Mrs. Moore's husband, Cyril, and Mrs. Cottrell's brother-in-law, Charles Cottrell, came to Osbrook Point in a lobster boat from Avondale, which is on the Rhode Island side of the Pawcatuck River. When their flashlights were seen from the Chase cabin, Mrs. Moore noted with some exasperation, George Chase was slow in flashing his kerosene lamp at the window as an answering signal, "but we forced him into it, he all the time saying, 'If they want somebody, they will knock.' The next thing I knew I heard a voice say, 'Hello, is anyone there?' My reaction to Charlie Cottrell's voice was a moment I will never live again, for I knew that Cy would be with him. We were simply speechless, all of us. It was too good to be true to find ourselves all together again."

In the morning they went to Avondale in the lobster boat. "Food and bed were heaven," Mrs. Moore said.

*   *   *   *

The party of eleven refugees from the Geoffrey Moore cottage, sailing across the hurricane-swept bay on the floor of the maid's room, landed to the west of Osbrook Point on Barn Island, a less fortunate place to come ashore not only because it was completely uninhabited and without any kind of a standing structure for shelter, not even an empty shack or a barn, but because the storm had isolated the island from the Connecticut mainland. A shallow stream between the north edge of the island and the mainland, usually only a few feet wide, had become a raging torrent almost 150 feet across. Jeff and Catherine Moore and their four young children; May Doherty; the maid and the cook, Loretta and Nancy; the young handy man, Andy; and Jim Nestor, the boy from the wrecked cottage next door, could only wait on the island without food, warmth, or shelter until somebody came by boat to rescue them. They would have paid any price that night for George Chase's little cabin, with its wood-burning stove, and a cup of Chase's hot ginger tea.

The only place on Barn Island where they could find some slight protection against the cold was in a stack of aged, stiff, scratchy, and dusty hay. The hay had once been stored in a barn, perhaps the barn that had given the island its name, but the barn had long since collapsed, leaving the stacked hay exposed to the weather for several years. "At the bottom of the haystack, there was a hollow place about six feet long and three feet deep," Catherine Moore wrote later in her letter to her brother. "This Jeff called the women's dormitory. We pulled down hay in front of this place while the men scooped out another place a few feet away which Jeff called the men's dormitory. The men decided to take the two younger children in with them, and Andy was given the job of keeping Margaret covered with hay and Jim took care of Cathy. Geoffrey [the family's twelve-year-old son, who had left Napatree Point wearing no shirt and refusing to put one on] took care of himself. I pitied him with that briery hay scratching his skin all night, but he had no complaint to make and was as helpful as could be."

Jeff Moore, despite having suffered a heart attack shortly before his cottage was swept off the beach at Napatree Point, stayed up all night as a lookout, walking around the shore and climbing to the top of the haystack to watch for the lights of a passing boat. "This was punishment for Jeff, with no shoes," his wife wrote. "The wind was cold and his woolen shirt had shrunk so that it no longer covered him. In the morning he was blue with cold. The five of us in the women's dormitory, May, Anne, Nancy, Loretta, and myself, lay down in the cubbyhole side by side. I could only get in up to my waist. We reached up and pulled more hay from overhead, but it was hard pulling and the briers scratched us. Hayseed and goodness only knows what else came down with the hay into our eyes. The stars came out and the wind died down. We could only watch the sky and listen for the sound of a motorboat or any other strange sound and stamp our feet to try to keep them warm. Once we thought we did hear a motor, and I acted as cheerleader and led two long *Helloooooooo*'s.

"We did this intermittently all night long. Of course, we

did not know that the catastrophe was so far-reaching. We thought that only the Fort Road had gone. We saw the reflection of a fire in the sky, and thought it must be in Stonington but it turned out later to have been New London. In one of Jeff's trips to the top of the haystack, he reported seeing flashlights on Osbrook Point. We felt a little more cheerful then because searching parties were out. We called and called, but after a while the lights disappeared."

Before dawn in the morning, several big black clouds came overhead, making Mrs. Moore fear another hurricane. "It seemed that we were so cold it would be humanly impossible to survive," she wrote later. "As soon as we could see clearly enough to distinguish objects, Jeff was up to take a look around and to do exercises to start the circulation in his chilled body. He reported not a boat in sight. Now new fears arose, How long would we have to stay there? Jeff urged us to get up and move about but we didn't feel much like moving. The sun came up, and Jeff and Geoffrey started to walk around the island, a slow and painful procedure because of the thorns and wreckage. The rest of us finally got up and exercised a little, and laughed to see that we were all covered with dirt from the hay, and our eyes and teeth stood out from the blackness of our faces. Our wet clothes looked as though they had been through a mud puddle."

Later in the morning Alvin Scott's lobster boat from Avondale, the same boat that had earlier rescued Jeff's brother's family from the Chase cabin on Osbrook Point, appeared off Barn Island. It took three trips in a rowboat to get the eleven people from the shore to the lobster boat, which could not get in close through the debris.

"If it had been the most palatial yacht ever to sail the seven seas, it couldn't have looked more beautiful to me than Mr.

Scott's boat did that morning," Mrs. Moore wrote. "We glanced over the bay at the place we had loved so much, the place we had often called Heaven on Earth. It just wasn't there. A strip of sand and a few telephone poles were all that remained to mark the place that was known as the Fort Road. I just want to say that during the whole thing no one lost his head. We were all calm. The first thing we did when we reached the haystack was to thank God, Who in such a miraculous manner had saved our lives. We were all most uncomfortable during that endless night, but no one complained. We even joked and laughed a little to keep our spirits up. The children were marvelous. When Margaret woke in the morning she asked what we were going to have for breakfast, and when I said she could help herself to a little hay, she only laughed. It is almost unbelievable, but not one of us even had a cold as a result of this whole experience."

After the storm the yacht club and the beach club with its cabanas and bathhouse pavilions were rebuilt on Napatree Point, but Fort Road and its long line of cottage dwellings have never been rebuilt. Vacationing families come to the beach on the point in beach buggies and boats and camp there overnight, and the survivors of the Fort Road disaster who still have summer homes at Watch Hill, such as the Moores and Helen Joy Lee, go there for swimming and sun-bathing, but nobody lives there any more. The emptiness of the beach on Napatree Point today is a far more striking reminder of the tragedy of the hurricane of 1938 than any monument could ever be.

*　　*　　*　　*

East of Napatree Point, along the twenty miles of Rhode Island coast between Watch Hill and Point Judith, there were other stretches of exposed and isolated ocean beaches, crowded with cottages, that offered no means of escape from the sudden massive surge of hurricane waves at the climax of the storm. Like Westhampton Beach and Napatree Point, these oceanside resorts at Misquamicut, Quonochontaug, Charlestown Beach, and Matunuck were built on outer sand bars, separated from the safer and higher ground of the mainland by wide expanses of water and swamps. The devastating surge of high water, piled up on the ocean east of Montauk Point, Long Island, by gales recorded at 120 miles per hour at the Watch Hill Coast Guard station, swept some of the beaches so clean, foundations and all, that owners of lost cottages were later unable to find their lots. The Red Cross, trying to check on missing persons after the storm, had to consult telephone company maps to find out where houses had been. The large beach resort at Misquamicut was almost completely destroyed; 369 cottages and several business buildings were leveled and 41 people drowned, including one group of 10 women who were attending a church picnic.

Two couples, who were next-door neighbors at Quonochontaug, the Charles Merritts and the Richard J. Smiths, ran to the only safe place in sight, the top of a small mound of high ground behind their cottages, when the rising waves covered their windows. The water followed them and climbed the hill too, steadily rising on all sides until the top of the hill, where the two men and the two women were standing closely huddled together, became a tiny island, only four feet square. The men and their wives waited, terrified, for the water to wipe out the remaining bit of dry land below them. "We could see animals trying to swim near us," Mrs. Smith said later. But the water stopped rising before it touched their feet, and after a long while it began to edge slowly down the sides of the hill.

East of Point Judith the foaming crest of high water rolled into Narragansett Bay with such force that it lifted from a breakwater jetty several big boulders, each weighing twenty tons, and moved them fifty feet. At Newport, the large island at the mouth of the bay, the surge of waves was high enough to wreck several of the palatial homes on the cliffs of Ocean Drive and to wash out the roadbed of the drive itself. The surf demolished the exclusive Bailey's Beach and the amusement park at Newport Beach and destroyed five hundred houses in a real-estate development on the Sakonnet River side of Newport. At one lowland section of the Newport shore, the startled people saw a huge, mile-wide wave sweep across two miles of inland fields before it smashed against a range of hills. At Jamestown the water covered a school bus, drowning seven children. A young crippled woman in a flooded cottage at Quonset Point begged her mother and her two sisters to leave her and run to safety; they refused, and three of them, the mother and the crippled daughter and one of her sisters, were killed.

As the towering tide charged up Narragansett Bay toward the unsuspecting cities of Providence, Rhode Island, and Fall River, Massachusetts—gaining force as it was squeezed between the narrowing upper shores of the thirty-mile waterway—it smashed and flooded such bayside towns as Portsmouth, Tiverton, North Kingstown, Bristol, Warren, and Warwick. At Oakland Beach on Warwick Cove, a Catholic priest, the Reverend Valmore G. Savignac, and a local high-school athlete, Edward Thompson, were shoring up a tree across the street from Father Savignac's rectory when a woman told them that the water from the bay was engulfing the houses on the waterfront. The two men ran to the flooded neighborhood and found a high wall of water rushing up the street toward them. They dived into it and swam to a house where a woman and her children were calling for help from an upstairs window. The water had already flooded the lower part of the house. Father Savignac found that the woman was an invalid. He grabbed a boat that was floating nearby, carried the woman to it, and then he and Thompson went back to the house and carried out the children. In another house, the priest found an elderly couple asleep in their bed with the water rising to the level of their mattress. The wife was crippled with rheumatism and unable to walk. Father Savignac and Thompson carried her out of the house on a chair.

One of the houses on Warwick Cove was ripped from its foundation by the surge of waves and turned over completely in the rolling surf with a woman and her two small children and their nursemaid inside it. "We were on a wall, then on the ceiling, and then on the floor again," Mrs. J. Wilfred Thereault, the mother of the children, said later." The house then started falling apart. The ceiling fell on us. We pushed it up with our hands and kept it from crushing us. I reached for the young baby and I hung him, by the back strap of his tiny overalls, on a big nail in a timber beam. I turned around to see how the older child was faring, and when I turned back, in just a moment, the piece of wreckage where the baby was hanging had drifted away. There was about ten feet of water between me and the baby hanging on the wreckage. I couldn't get to him." That evening Mrs. Thereault and her older child and the nursemaid floated ashore on the wrecked house a mile upstream from its foundations. The baby's body was found the next morning.

At the head of Narragansett Bay, the hurricane-driven surge of water from the ocean rushed into the Taunton River to the Massachusetts mill city of Fall River, and up the Providence and Seekonk rivers, the waterways that run between Providence and East Providence. An oil tanker, loaded with 57,000 gallons of gasoline, was torn from its mooring at Fall River and carried five miles upstream in the Taunton River to Somerset, hitting the riverbank nine times in its wild journey. A young woman named Mary Haggerty, who was working alone in a small office building on the Providence waterfront near the old dry dock, looked out a window and saw that she was floating on the Seekonk River. She ran upstairs to the roof, and as the building was swept along the river to the India Point Bridge, she reached up, grabbed the bridge rail, and hung from it until she was rescued by a group of men in a lifeboat who had just escaped from a sinking tugboat.

The water rushed from the head of the Providence River into the streets of the downtown business district around City Hall and the Biltmore Hotel; it was late in the afternoon, a time when the city was crowded with shoppers and when people were still at work in offices and stores. The flood rose almost two feet above the bronze tablet on the wall of the old market house that marked the height of the hurricane flood in 1815: 11 feet, 9¾ inches. People ran from the fast-rising water to the upper floors of stores and office buildings. Motorists climbed to the roofs of submerged automobiles. The headlights of many of the cars were shining under the water and gave the flood a strange glow; hundreds of short-circuited automobile horns blew steadily, starting a deafening din all over the city. Some victims who were trapped on sidewalks in water up to their necks were hauled up to fire escape ladders on the sides of buildings. In movie theaters, as the lights went out and the water swirled into the orchestra-level seats, people ran upstairs to the balconies. One of the two hundred people who took shelter in the Grace Episcopal Church when the flood poured into Westminster

Street said later, "It was an eerie scene in the church as the flickering candles on the altar and in the side chapel gave the only light on the shadowy forms crowded into the pews."

One of the people trapped in Providence during the storm was F. Van Wyck Mason, the author of popular historical novels. He had unfortunately picked that Wednesday to travel from his summer home at Nantucket to New York, to deliver to his publisher the seven-hundred-page manuscript of a novel that he had just completed after a year and a half of work. The steamboat ferry that carried Mason from Nantucket ran into the early gales and surf of the hurricane near New Bedford, where it missed its dock and crashed into another pier. Finding no trains or planes running out of New Bedford, Mason took a bus from there to Providence. Between New Bedford and Fall River a flaming electric wire fell across the bus, and two trees fell across the road in front of it, but the driver managed to get his passengers into Providence. When Mason was leaving the bus, the bricks of a chimney fell at his feet. Holding the brief case containing his precious manuscript above his head as protection against other falling objects, the author hurried to the railroad station in Providence, seeking a train to New York. Just as he reached the station, its roof blew off with a roar.

Standing in the door of the roofless terminal, Mason saw the water rising to a height of more than ten feet in the central square below the station and watched a woman drowning in the racing flood as she tried to climb out of her sinking automobile. "I saw another woman wading to safety when she suddenly dropped out of sight," he said.

Another writer, the late poet and novelist David Cornel De Jong, was also marooned in downtown Providence by the hurricane, and later wrote for *Yankee* magazine a vivid account of what he saw in the wind-swept and flooded city. Before the flood, De Jong took shelter from the rain in a shopping arcade between Westminster and Weybosset streets. Open at both ends, the arcade became a dangerous tunnel of wind as the gales blew harder.

"Somebody bellowed that the arcade was a natural air pocket and that we'd all perish there," De Jong wrote. "With four others I ran, somehow, in the general direction of home, while beside us a plate-glass window lunged toward us and crashed, and hard, stinging debris hailed upon us. Just ahead of us an old woman had her neck sliced by a pane of glass; she tumbled, straightened herself, bent her head, and brunting the storm, went on, leaving a trail of blood behind her. When we reached her, her hair and dress were sodden with blood, but she wouldn't believe it. . . .

"Then the wind stopped us. It was like an invisible wall in front of us, holding us impotently suspended, but spattering the woman's blood over our faces. Then, while we grabbed the woman, it madly pushed us into a nearby revolving door. With the door we turned, two and three in each compartment, and were deposited in a crowded lobby, where a crowd laughed at us foolishly, until they saw the injured woman. Then girls screamed and shut their eyes, and men folded their arms protectingly around them. No one seemed to know what to do with the woman, everybody stood and stared until a practical waitress decided to do something about that awful dripping blood. The old woman herself sat there wide-eyed and smiling."

A few minutes later De Jong and the other people in the crowded lobby of the office building saw the swirling, white-capped water rising on the street outside, and found the sight of such a sudden flood in their downtown shopping district hard to believe. The water rushed through the revolving door into the lobby and everybody ran to the stairs. De Jong came upon a lawyer friend, who led him to his firm's offices on the third floor of the building.

De Jong ran to a window in the law office to watch the tidal wave, as one of the lawyers had called it. "Directly below us an old man, neck deep in water, lifted his hands and sank," De Jong wrote later. "We craned our necks, but never saw him again. He was drowned. 'Must have been drunk, the crazy fool,' three men said simultaneously. But their eyes said: he couldn't have been drowned, not there, our eyes are crazy. The men turned away from the window, all three, and lighted cigarettes."

De Jong continued to watch from the window while a group of people sat near him, wisecracking and telling jokes as they tried to make candles with dental wax from a dentist's office a few doors down the hall. He saw a blonde-haired lady dummy from a dress shop window floating in the street: "Holding her head high, her visage vacant, never sinking, [she] pirouetted on the flood like a well-mannered debutante." A desk floated by, with the handle of a pencil sharpener on one of its corners turning in the wind. Bright red tennis balls came out of a broken store window "like puffed exotic fish."

Then other people in the office crowded beside De Jong at the window to stare at a group of sixteen people, up to their chins in water, who were trying to make an escape from a flooded store. They formed a chain, each one clutching the persons before and behind him, as they struggled through the water. The one at the end of the chain, a hysterical woman, lost her grip and fell behind the others. Three times the other people in the group returned to the weeping woman patiently and re-formed the chain with her linked to their grasp, only to have her break away again and again. De Jong heard somebody beside him saying, "They ought to spank her." Finally the chain of people remained intact long enough to reach a place of safety. Then De Jong heard a shout, "Look at the blonde!"

"The blonde dummy had tilted her head through a store window," he wrote, "and seemed to be peering haughtily inside. Suddenly an enormous beam rushed upon her and crushed her. At the sight of it, the girls screamed, and then we all laughed. And as if they were a little ashamed of themselves, most of them returned to the slow task of candlemaking. 'Oh, gee,' a girl said. 'Oh, gee, I wonder what my mother is thinking.' At last we had one candle and sat around it. The telephone seemed dead except for one incoming call: a wife demanding to know every fifteen minutes why her husband didn't come home. He simply had to; their elm had fallen down. She didn't believe for a minute that we were all marooned in thirteen feet of water."

Later, in the darkness, De Jong watched from the window a repulsive aftermath of the disaster, the arrival of the looters. "They came neck deep or swimming," he wrote, "holding flashlights dry above them, rising out of the water and disappearing through demolished store windows. At first there were a few, then there were hordes, assisting each other. They seemed organized, almost regimented, as if they'd daily drilled and prepared for this event, the like of which hadn't happened in a hundred and twenty years. They were brazen and insatiable; they swarmed like rats; they took everything. When a few policemen came past in a rowboat, they didn't stop their looting. They knew they outnumbered the police; besides, the latter were intent on rescue work."

That night, as deer and elk that had escaped from the wrecked local zoo roamed Roger Williams Park in Providence, the downtown streets of the city were lit up by the glare of big searchlights mounted on trucks of National Guard antiaircraft units to combat the blackout caused by the hurricane. Van Wyck Mason managed to find refuge in the old and exclusive Hope Club, where he sat up all night in candlelight with the manuscript of his new novel on his lap. "For the first time in the history of the club," Mason said later, "women were admitted within the doors—women refugees, of course. The oldsters at the club didn't like it. They said no good would come of it."

* * * *

On the south shore of New England, east of Narragansett Bay, the Massachusetts seaside resorts along the usually safe and sheltered sailing waters of Buzzards Bay were the next targets to be hit by the lofty, power-packed surge of waves that the vicious gales on the eastern back side of the rotating hurricane had been pushing across the ocean from Cape Hatteras. Buzzards Bay slants toward the northeast between New Bedford and Martha's Vineyard, indenting the coast line so deeply that it almost cuts off Cape Cod from the rest of Massachusetts. Its wide mouth swallowed a choking gulp of the steeply towering wall of foaming surf, probably rising more than thirty feet high as it jammed into the expanse of the lower bay; the water was still rolling at heights of more than fifteen feet when it covered waterfront docks and smashed the main streets of towns near the Cape Cod Canal at the head of the bay, thirty miles from the ocean. Even beyond the bay, farther inland on the Wareham River, the hurricane wave was high enough to lift up a boat with a man in it and carry it over a bridge.

The sudden and completely unexpected surge of water from

the ocean brought terror and destruction and death to every shorefront town on the bay. At the bay-shore estate of William O. Taylor, publisher of the Boston *Globe*, near the south end of the Cape Cod Canal, Mr. and Mrs. Taylor decided to move their family and servants from their house when surf began to break over the top of a high sea wall on their beach. The family, including several small children, were heading for the Taylors' garage on higher ground behind the house when they were engulfed in a shoulder-high flood of waves. Two of the maids, Margaret May and Rose Collins, were carried away from the others and were drowned. Mrs. May's body was found later a mile away from the Taylor estate, beyond the railroad tracks in the town of Buzzards Bay. At the nearby shorefront community of Gray Gables, a man named Hayward Wilson went to the summer home of Mrs. John Lane to warn her and her three house guests that the water on the bay was getting high. While Wilson was urging Mrs. Lane to go to a safer location, the house was swept into the Cape Cod Canal and smashed against an abutment of the Bourne Bridge, killing all five people in it. The water from the bay rose so quickly that a man in one town near it ran across a street in a flood up to his ankles to rescue a small child from a parked automobile, and made his way back from the car, carrying the child, through waves that reached his chest.

At Onset a crowd of several hundred townspeople ran to the top of the one and only sizable hill in the area and were marooned there for several hours. At Mattapoisett a chauffeur and a cook from the summer home of Dr. Austen Riggs, a nationally known psychiatrist, were trapped in an automobile by the waves; the chauffeur climbed to the roof of the car, where he held the sixty-nine-year-old cook by her arms for more than two hours before she was carried away from his grasp and drowned. Mrs. Parker Converse strapped her six-year-old son to her back and swam to higher ground from her flooded cottage on Blake's Point at Marion. On the shore road at Falmouth, on the Cape Cod side of Buzzards Bay, a small boy left his aunt in her stalled car and went to a house a half mile away to get help. The aunt was never seen again; the empty automobile was found, a hundred yards from where he had left it, under water in Salt Pond.

The east side of Buzzards Bay and the west shore of the nearby island of Martha's Vineyard marked the end of the stretch of New England coast terrorized by the surge of hurricane waves; Cape Cod beyond the Cape Cod Canal, the east side of Martha's Vineyard, and Nantucket were outside the circle of intense hurricane gales, too far east from the center of the whirlwinds for the surf to be extremely high and destructive. But the hurricane was far from exhausted when it left the ocean and roared on to the north across the attractively wet and humid farmlands and swaying forests of Massachusetts, New Hampshire, and Vermont. Meteorologists noted in later studies of the hurricane's behavior that as it traveled inland over western Massachusetts and Vermont, the low-pressure area of its eye stretched to a length of 50 miles along its north-south axis, with destructive gales extending only a short distance to the west of the eye. But the rotating gales on the stronger east side of the eye remained extremely powerful over a distance of 100 miles from the center. Gusts were recorded at a force of 186 miles per hour both at Harvard's weather observatory at the Blue Hills near Boston and at the summit of Mount Washington, in New Hampshire's White Mountains, where the trestle of the Jacob's Ladder cogwheel scenic railway was torn down.

The gales did widespread damage in Boston, although no

deaths were reported in the city. The spectators' stands at Harvard's varsity baseball diamond, beside the Harvard Stadium, were torn from their concrete foundations and moved nine feet to the west. The historic steeple on the Old North Church, where signal lanterns were hung to start Paul Revere on his midnight ride, swayed dangerously but did not fall. (The steeple was to collapse in a later and almost identical New England hurricane, the one named Carol in 1954.) The frigate *Constitution*, better known as *Old Ironsides*, was badly battered at her dock in the Boston Navy Yard. Elliot Norton, the Boston drama critic, recalled a moving moment during the height of the hurricane in Back Bay. Making his way along Huntington Avenue, Norton was surprised and touched to hear the chimes in the Christian Science Mother Church "bravely and beautifully" playing "Onward Christian Soldiers."

The hurricane did its worst damage in Massachusetts across the central part of the state. In Worcester the gales tore the steeples off five churches, ripped the roof from the Classical High School, and started several fires in wrecked buildings. A man named James Howe, who was closing a window in the Worcester Processed Steel Company industrial plant, was pulled through the window by a gust of wind and thrown to the ground fifteen feet below; he died of a fractured skull. The storm left two hundred families homeless in Orange, where tapioca from a demolished factory filled the Athol River. The small manufacturing town of Ware was inundated by a sudden flood from the swollen Ware River. An express train, bound for Boston from Chicago by way of Albany, was stopped on the flooded tracks at West Brookfield and remained stranded there for the next twenty-four hours.

Roaring north into New Hampshire, the storm started a

fire in Peterboro that raged all through the night, leveling five buildings in the center of the town, where the streets were flooded by five feet of water from the overflowing Contoocook River. One of the most severely damaged towns in New Hampshire was East Weare on the Piscataquog River near Concord. The downpour of rain from the hurricane raised the river and changed its course so that it flowed through the main street of East Weare, dividing the village in two; groceries and mail had to be carried across the flooded street in baskets on ropes strung through pulleys. East Weare's three small industrial buildings, a toy factory, a creamery plant, and a lumber mill, were all destroyed, and the village suffered damages amounting, at the low prices of 1938, to a staggering $350,000.

About nine o'clock that Wednesday night, when the gales around the center of the hurricane over the Green Mountains south of Burlington, Vermont, were shifting from the east to the south, the campus at Dartmouth College in Hanover, New Hampshire, was battered almost as badly as the campus at Yale in New Haven had been at four o'clock in the afternoon. A story was told later about a prefabricated house that a young married couple had assembled in New Hampshire as a vacation home. When the hurricane came into northern New England, the man and his wife were relaxing after dinner at their mountain retreat, unaware that the storm outside was particularly unusual. The lights went out and suddenly the walls and the roof of the house disappeared into the dark sky, leaving only the floor and the two unharmed occupants. The missing prefabricated sections of the house were never found, although a careful search for them was made in the surrounding countryside.

In Vermont, the most rural and sparsely populated of the New England states, the biggest damage done by the hurricane was the destruction of two thirds of the state's cherished sugar maple trees. Such Vermont cities and towns as Montpelier, St. Johnsbury, Barre, and Burlington were hard hit by the gales. A gannet, an ocean bird whose habitat is the North Atlantic, was carried into East Corinth, near Barre, by the hurricane, and several yellow-billed tropical birds native to the West Indies were found elsewhere in Vermont.

About ten o'clock that night, six hours after it had come ashore on Long Island, the center of the hurricane passed over Lake Champlain, where a few boats were sunk or thrown ashore, and moved on into Canada. By then the storm was dissipating and losing power, but its gales were still strong enough to do some serious damage at Montreal, where the cyclonic whirlwinds were last felt and reported. From there the remains of the hurricane drifted off to northern Ontario and died.

4

O N THE BRIGHT and sunny day after the hurricane of 1938,
when the village center at Westhampton Beach on Long Island
was filled with scores of bewildered dogs trying to find their
missing homes and owners, most of New England was cut off
from the rest of the United States. All over the hurricane-
crippled area, telephone and telegraph communication was
blacked out and railroads and highways were blocked by storm
damage. Urgent messages from New York to eastern New England were sent to London and Paris and relayed back across the
Atlantic to wireless and cable receiving stations on eastern Cape
Cod, which had escaped the brunt of the hurricane. Postmaster
General James A. Farley borrowed a Navy battleship, the U.S.S.
Wyoming, to carry mail between New York and Boston.

   Providence's only communication with the outside world,
and even with stricken towns within Rhode Island, was through
short-wave radio messages, which were mostly sent and received
by amateur operators. Milk from Vermont had to be shipped to

Boston by way of Montreal and Maine. A Coast Guard chief with a Lyle gun, used to fire lines to crippled ships at sea, was flown from Rockaway, Long Island, to Massachusetts to help restore long-distance telephone cables that had been broken by the washout of a bridge across the swollen Chicopee River at Chicopee Falls. A nineteen-pound projectile, attached to a line that was designed to pull new cables, was successfully fired seven hundred feet across the river, although unfortunately it crashed through the roof of a laundry plant on the other side.

Mostly because of the communications black-out, but partly because the idea of such a widespread tropical hurricane on Long Island and in New England then seemed incredible, a full realization of the enormity of the disaster was slow in emerging. Like a difficult jigsaw puzzle, the whole picture took a few days to piece together. News of what had happened in various localities was hard to get. People in many wrecked towns did not learn until later in the week that the storm had been a hurricane and that it had hit not only their own immediate area but several states. *The New York Times* knew so little about the extent of the destruction that the day after the hurricane it gave the front-page headline to the war crisis in Czechoslovakia. Not until the second day after the disaster, when scattered reports began to show that it was a worse catastrophe than the Chicago fire, the San Francisco earthquake, or the Mississippi floods of 1927, did the *Times* hasten to devote banner headlines to the hurricane.

The New England newspapers were also slow in getting the details. The Boston *Globe* was luckier than its competitors in obtaining on Friday a description of the disaster area by Harrison McDonald, a traveler from the Midwest who had spent Wednesday, Thursday, and Friday morning making his way from Albany to Boston by train and taxicab. McDonald made better time than a group of passengers who left New York City on Wednesday on a bus headed for Portland, Maine, and did not arrive at their destination until Friday night. There was also a group of five Massachusetts supreme court judges who had been trying since Wednesday to make the one-hundred-mile trip from Springfield to Boston. They finally made it on Friday night in a National Guard truck convoy after a highway route across Massachusetts was opened for urgent traffic.

McDonald had little to tell the Boston *Globe* about the hurricane itself, which he had sat out in comparative comfort on a detoured New York Central express train, the Wolverine, near New London. He was, however, able to give Boston readers their first detailed account of conditions in Connecticut and Rhode Island on the day after the storm.

"A good-sized steamship has been thrown up on the railroad station's tracks in New London," McDonald said. "I don't mean a yacht or a tug. I mean a steamship. I was standing at the desk in the Western Union office in New London on the afternoon after the storm when a girl came in there. She was looking for her younger sister, who has not been heard of since school let out at almost the moment the tidal wave hit on Wednesday afternoon.

"The clerk said they had no report on her, and a moment later a businessman came in.

" 'Can I get a wire through to New York?' he asked.

" 'No.'

" 'Well, I don't suppose it's essential,' he said. 'I'd like to let my company in New York know they haven't got any New London factory any more. It's not a problem of damage, but one of complete abolition.' "

McDonald had left Albany on the Wolverine at six o'clock

in the morning on Wednesday, the day of the hurricane, expecting to reach Boston, by way of Springfield and Worcester on the Boston and Albany Railroad line, two hours later. At Springfield the train was detoured south to Connecticut because of flood washouts. Its new route would take it to Hartford and New Haven and then on to Boston by way of New London and Providence.

The train made its way slowly to Hartford with floods from the rising Connecticut River lapping at the tracks. At 3:15 in the afternoon, when the hurricane gales were blowing hard across Long Island Sound, the train came to a halt on the shore about three miles west of New London.

"The engineer, a smart fellow, pulled to a sharp curve in the track and stopped there," McDonald said. "He figured the curve of the cars against the wind would help us, and I guess it did. I don't think that train could have stayed upright if it was broadside to the wind in a straight line. A Pullman car weighs sixty-seven tons, and, as it was, the cars were rocking, not just shivering or shaking, but literally rocking. The Yankee Clipper, the one o'clock express from New York to Boston, pulled up behind us and we spent the night there. We were comfortable and had plenty to eat, but the trains ran out of water, and finally they were passing coal from the engine back to the dining car in order to keep the fire going and cook food.

"The next morning we were taken into New London in buses. The first thing we were given was a card from the National Guardsmen—the city is under martial law—warning us not to drink water or milk without boiling it. The first store I saw was a five-and-ten-cent one. It had been flooded out, but one counter had been set up on the sidewalk and it was selling candles only.

"We went to the railroad station and saw that good-sized steamer resting there. We walked down to the business district and found firemen still pouring water into the smoldering embers. They said that the fire had raged all night, and it seemed to have leveled about ten blocks. It followed in the wake of the tidal wave.

"Almost everyone in the city seemed to have experienced disaster. Parents were crowding the newspaper office and the police station in search of school children—they had been missing for eighteen hours by then and little hope was held for them. Officials told us school had let out just before the flood.

"One man had managed to get forty girls out of his factory after the wind had lifted the roof off it and a moment before the flood and the fire hit it. Another had several missing from his factory still, and the factory was gone. All over New London we saw trees uprooted, and many of them had crashed through automobiles and houses. All the waterfront was demolished by the flood tide, and boats, large and small, were scattered along the streets. The editor of the New London *Day* told me six miles of waterfront property was completely wrecked. He said a hundred or more summer cottages were swept to sea in five minutes at Ocean Beach."

That Thursday night the railroad hired a taxicab to take McDonald and a few other passengers from the stopped train to Providence, where they arrived about eleven o'clock. During the day in downtown Providence groups of foraging youngsters had been picking through piles of wet merchandise in the gutters outside flood-soaked stores, and arrangements had been made to transport $31,000,000 in cash, including seven tons of silver coins, in a convoy of armored trucks from Providence banks to the Federal Reserve Bank in Boston for safekeeping during the post-hurricane emergency period.

"Providence was like a city in wartime," McDonald said. "The entire business district that night was roped off and patrolled by armed soldiers. Huge antiaircraft lights pierced the night. As you registered at the Hotel Biltmore, you saw a sign reminding you to take a candle with you. You had to climb to your room as well, since the elevators weren't running. Food was rationed. The bars were closed. The next morning we came over the road to Boston. You don't know how queer it seems to be in a normal city with lights, heat, and telephones running. It seemed a month since we last enjoyed these luxuries."

*   *   *   *

The good-sized steamer that Harrison McDonald had seen lying across the railroad tracks in New London was a three-hundred-foot government lighthouse tender. It stayed there for a week after the hurricane while the railroad complained that the ship could not be moved without a permit from the government. On the day after the storm the New Haven Railroad also estimated that 1,200 trees and 700 telegraph poles were lying across its tracks; almost thirty miles of tracks and roadbeds between New London and Providence on its Shore Line had to be completely rebuilt. The Shore Line, the main passenger line between New York and Boston, was not reopened for through-train service until October 8. Mexican workers from Texas were brought north to help on the rush job. All the railroads in New England were under pressure to repair hurricane damage as soon as possible so that urgently needed building materials, and mechanical parts for industrial machinery broken by the storm, could be delivered to the region by freight trains. One bridge, still under repair, had freight trains moving over it while it was being held up temporarily by a giant crane.

The breakdown of transportation, communications, and electric power disrupted business, industry, and social activity after the hurricane. Movie theaters were closed. In the more battered and crippled cities and towns early curfews were enforced. At a time when newspapers were hard to find and radio news was desperately needed, the radios in most homes were silent; the average home radio in 1938 was powered through a wall socket. In some localities the lack of news started disturbing rumors of the approach of another hurricane, false reports of an outbreak of war in Europe, and frighteningly exaggerated tales of storm disasters in nearby towns.

During the emergency period after the hurricane, when Rhode Island was under martial law, National Guard troops barred sight-seers from visiting wrecked shorefront resorts. The restriction, designed to prevent looting, started wild rumors in Westerly, a few miles inland from Watch Hill, that all the people on that section of the ocean coast had been killed by the hurricane waves. One false report from Westerly, printed in the New York *Herald Tribune* and other out-of-state newspapers, said that two hundred persons had been washed into the ocean from the top of a high sand dune at Watch Hill. The story brought anxious inquiries by short-wave radio from all over the United States. On the day after the hurricane, Marcelle and Sally Hammond, daughters of Charles Hammond, the publisher of Watch Hill's weekly *Seaside Topics*, drove from New York to find out how their parents had fared during the storm. The Hammond house at Watch Hill, which was on high ground a safe distance from the ocean, had been badly damaged but it had remained intact, and Hammond and his wife were both unhurt.

Arriving that Thursday night in Westerly, the Hammond girls stopped for gasoline at a service station in the center of the town and asked the man who was operating the powerless pump by hand how things were at Watch Hill.

"Watch Hill?" the service-station man said. "There's nothing left in Watch Hill. All the people are gone."

Distraught with grief and shock, the two girls went to the home of their family doctor in Westerly to learn what he might know of their parents' death. They were assured by the doctor that both their father and mother were safe and well.

Westerly, the largest town in a devastated coastal area where 112 people had died, had no facility for calling outside help after its telephone and telegraph lines and electric power were completely knocked out during the hurricane. Two local amateur radio operators, Will Burgess and George Marshall, rigged up a battery-powered short-wave transmitter a few hours after the storm and sent out QRR distress signals, the land equivalent of an SOS, which were picked up by the Red Cross headquarters in Washington. The Red Cross contacted Rhode Island state officials and the state National Guard command in Providence and gave them the first news of the destruction in the Westerly area.

In Providence, on the night of the storm, a group of volunteer ham operators established an emergency short-wave radio station in Room 229 in the State House, next to Governor Robert E. Quinn's office. With twenty-five amateur operators working in shifts around the clock, Station W1INM in the candlelit Room 229 handled more than two thousand official messages for the state government and personal inquiries about missing or unreachable persons during the next few days. There were calls from hard pressed undertakers in shorefront towns asking Providence funeral directors to send them embalmers, calls from hospitals for vaccines and X-ray supplies, calls from the telephone company asking local police to guide repair crews traveling to Rhode Island from Midwestern and Southern states, calls from Army and Navy officers in Hawaii and the Panama Canal Zone asking if their wives and families in Newport, Pawtucket, or New London were safe. Messages from outside the state were relayed from the State House to police or amateur short-wave stations near the address and delivered from there by volunteer messengers. Many of the messengers were Boy Scouts, who also delivered water and food in stricken communities, helped in clearing debris, and directed detoured traffic.

One message from California directed to a man in the Westerly area said, "Let us know if you are dead or alive." At a particularly busy hour on the night after the hurricane, when urgent government messages were waiting to be transmitted, there was a call to Providence from the Animal Rescue League in Massachusetts, announcing that a black setter, with the name of a resident of Saunderstown, Rhode Island, on its collar, had been found in Worcester. One of the amateur operators in Providence—who received no pay for their work—remarked later that it was not until Tuesday night in the week after the storm that he found enough time to send a message to his own son in Wyoming saying that the young man's parents had survived the hurricane without injury.

Heroic service after the storm was performed by two young married couples in Longmeadow, Massachusetts, Mr. and Mrs. Henry E. Stowell and Mr. and Mrs. Raymond Morrison, who kept a short-wave radio station in the Stowell home in continuous operation for five days and five nights after the hurricane. The Stowells' radio equipment was supplied with electric power because Longmeadow, a residential suburb near Springfield, had underground conduits that had remained in service during the hurricane. A few hours after the storm, Mrs. Stowell picked up the first news of the sudden flood that had destroyed and isolated the nearby factory town of Ware, Massachusetts. She heard of the Ware disaster from an amateur operator in Texas who had received a distress signal from the stricken town. Mrs. Stowell transmitted a call for help to state authorities in Boston, and for the rest of the week she and her husband and their next-door neighbors, the Morrisons, stayed up day and night receiving and sending emergency messages. On the Sunday morning after the storm, twenty-six-year-old Mrs. Stowell managed to get her first sleep since Wednesday, but she was awakened by a call from the adjutant general of the Massachusetts National Guard in Boston, asking her to get word to Ware that serum was to be dropped there from a plane later in the day. She got out of bed and sent the message.

When the commercial AM radio stations in the stricken areas were able to get back into operation, they devoted their time on the air to announcements concerning dead and missing persons and names of survivors. One radio station in Providence, WPRO, which had had its transmitting tower blown down, managed to resume broadcasting by hiring a farmer's tractor and connecting its engine to a power generator.

The search for missing persons and the task of trying to compile an accurate list of the known dead went on for several weeks. After the storm a young woman was found sitting alone on a wrecked dock at Ocean Beach on Fire Island. She explained quietly that she and her mother had been running, hand in hand, to catch the last boat leaving the beach during the hurricane. A huge storm wave from the ocean washed over them, sweeping the mother away. The daughter had turned back from the departing boat and had been wandering on the beach looking for her mother ever since.

Two days after the hurricane a woman who seemed to be calm and composed came to the office of a weekly newspaper on eastern Long Island and asked to place an advertisement in the lost and found column. The notice, which she had written carefully, asked for the return of her husband, who had been lost on the day of the storm.

A long search was made for the body of a pilot after a Navy plane was found wrecked and empty on Conanicut Island in Narragansett Bay; a later investigation showed that nobody had been in the plane—it had been carried through the air, empty, from the airport at the Newport naval training station to the island. (Similarly, an American Airlines plane, standing empty at Logan Airport in Boston, had been blown a mile away.)

Police at Center Moriches, Long Island, were puzzled not to find the body of Mrs. Donald Black in the wreckage of her house, where she had been at the time of the hurricane. As Mrs. Black explained later, she had been knocked unconscious when her house collapsed. Several hours later she awoke to find herself in a nearby woods and had gone from there to the empty home of a neighbor, where she stayed until the next day. A man in Island Park, Rhode Island, missing for twenty-four hours after the storm, was found unhurt under eight feet of debris.

The makeshift temporary morgues in high-school gymnasiums, dance halls, and armories held unidentified bodies for several days after the hurricane, and many of the missing persons presumed to be dead turned up later in cities far away, unaware that they had been reported lost. On the first reported list of the dead in Connecticut was Elmer Davis, the radio news commentator, who, like many others on the list, had not been in Connecticut that day. Two boys who were reported missing from an exclusive boarding school at Portsmouth, Rhode Island, appeared sheepishly at their homes in New York the next day. They had happened to pick the day of the hurricane to run away from school.

The list of the known dead, assumed dead, and missing persons in the Westerly shore area was revised almost hourly during the week after the storm. On Sunday, September 25, 71 were counted as dead and 46 as missing. By October 1, there were 109 known dead and 13 missing, and a week later, on October 8, when the list of known dead reached its final count of 112, the remaining 6 missing persons were accounted for and removed from the list. One of the six, Mrs. Louis Kingsbury, was found to be alive and well at her home in South Coventry, Connecticut, and the other five names were declared to be errors. The last of the fifteen victims killed in the Napatree Point disaster, Miss Havilla Moore of Staten Island, New York, was not found until twelve days after the hurricane. One of the survivors from Napatree Point, Ronald M. Byrnes of New York, lost his wife and his two daughters, Barbara and Betty, in the destruction at the beach. Barbara's body was still missing on the following Tuesday, when the funeral services for Mrs. Byrnes and Betty were to be held. A few hours before the double funeral was to begin, Barbara's body was found, and three caskets, instead of two, were carried into the church.

Not until October 1, ten days after the hurricane, was it reported that two scallop-fishing boats from Brooklyn had been sunk by the storm off Nantucket with eighteen men aboard. The Italian neighborhood at the North End of Boston, where many of the local fishermen made their homes, was a scene of grief and anxiety on the night after the hurricane when six boats, carrying thirty men from that district, were presumed to be missing at sea. Wives and children waited up all night at the small corner variety stores where messages for the neighborhood families were received at pay telephones, while older boys stood watch at the piers where the sturdy forty-foot boats of the Italian fishing fleet were berthed.

There was an outbreak of excitement and anguish on the North End streets during the night when one of the missing fishermen, Frank Marino, appeared at his home on Prince Street, weak and exhausted after having been rescued from the ocean outside Boston Harbor. His boat had capsized in the hurricane-driven waves with his brother, Tony Marino, and two other North End fishermen aboard. Frank Marino had been picked up by an outbound British freighter and transferred to an incoming trawler, which had landed at the Boston Fish Pier.

At dawn the next morning all the Italian boats in Boston went out to sea to search for the other missing fishing craft, and crowds of women and children gathered on the docks to await their return. They cheered loudly when one of the missing boats, the *Anna Madra*, chugged into the harbor about ten o'clock, badly damaged from the storm but with its crew of four men unhurt. Later in the morning the news came trickling in from other ports along the coast—Gloucester, Portsmouth, Provincetown, and Plymouth—that the rest of the survivors were safely ashore.

*　*　*　*

After the storm, when the streets were still blocked by fallen trees and wreckage, President Franklin D. Roosevelt in Washington sent his public works administrator, Harry Hopkins, to make a survey of the hurricane damage in New England and ordered the WPA, the Army, the Civilian Conservation Corps, and the Coast Guard to put one hundred thousand men to work immediately on clearing the storm-swept area and aiding its distressed victims. The Red Cross began a fund-raising drive for hurricane relief, and Congress considered an extensive program for rebuilding roads and destroyed waterfronts.

The task of providing relief for homeless survivors was enormous. More than twelve hundred cots, with blankets and bedding, had to be shipped to the town of Warwick, Rhode Island, alone, and the Red Cross gave shelter and food to 15,107 persons in the flooded cities of Hartford, Springfield, and Chicopee. With water supplies jeopardized, such bottled beverages as soda and beer became necessities, and the state of Rhode Island invoked emergency measures to stop a threatened strike of truck drivers who delivered beer. Sprinkler trucks from the race track at Narragansett Park carried water to disaster areas on the Rhode Island shore and to Coast Guard ships, which transported it to the fishing colony on Block Island, where water storage tanks had been wrecked in the storm.

The economic aspect of the disaster was staggering; many factories in New England, already shaken by the Depression of the 1930's, closed their doors and went out of business after the hurricane rather than attempting to pay for the rehabilitation of their damaged plants. Having experienced no big hurricane in the previous century, thrifty New Englanders had been reluctant to buy insurance against such a storm. The National Board of Fire Underwriters estimated that less than 5 per cent of the hurricane damage was covered by insurance; of the $38,000,000 paid nationally for windstorm protection in 1937, only $137,000 came from New England. On the day after the hurricane many small-business men, particularly fishermen and farmers, were left with a bleak outlook. At Block Island, for example, thirty-six of the fifty-six fishing boats were lost or sunk and the rest were badly damaged; most of the nets and other fishing equipment were gone. Lobster fishermen at the Biblically named ports of Galilee and Jerusalem, near Point Judith, reported that lobster traps 125 feet below the surface of the ocean 25 miles offshore had been smashed to splinters. All over the hurricane-hit states, widows with wrecked homes, and families whose wage earners were dead or injured, found themselves in hard straits.

Along with providing emergency shelter, food, and medical attention for victims of hurricanes, the Red Cross is authorized to offer financial aid, not as a loan but as a gift, to people striving to regain their self-sufficiency after having been economically stricken by such a natural disaster. The Red Cross reported that it found the traditionally proud New England Yankees reluctant to accept such help, even in cases where the sudden financial loss caused by the hurricane, coming on top of seven years of business depression, seemed to be the last straw. One case cited in the Red Cross report on the hurricane was that of a young married couple with a small baby who were left homeless by the storm. Their rented house, knocked off its foundation, was condemned as unsafe to enter. The couple were penniless; the twenty-two-year-old husband had been unemployed for eight months and the wife had been working as a waitress to pay for their food and rent. She had saved her tips to buy a baby carriage for their child, and the carriage had been blown away in the hurricane. They could not afford to replace the carriage. The Red Cross could have provided them with a place to live, at least temporarily, but they would accept nothing except another baby carriage.

"Really, lady, we can get along just fine ourselves if you will just get us another baby buggy or something for little Robert to sleep in," the young woman said to the Red Cross caseworker. "The baby has to sleep on a pillow. It's making him awful restless and he disturbs the others—you see, we're staying with some neighbors—and besides I don't think it's very healthy."

The Red Cross was able to do more for an older single woman whose predicament after the hurricane had seemed hopeless. She had been supporting herself by doing laundry work in the summer months at a beach vacation colony where she owned a small house, her only asset. She earned enough money from her summer work to pay the taxes on the house and to cover her expenses in the winter while she stayed with a nephew in a nearby town. When the hurricane struck, she was forced to flee from her house, which was later completely destroyed by a storm wave. As she ran out of the house, she grabbed the two hundred dollars that she had saved from her work during the summer. To save herself when she was engulfed by the storm wave, she dropped the money and threw her arms around a telephone pole. Although the woman survived the storm, she had lost her home, her savings, and her means of earning a livelihood. The Red Cross built a new house for her, furnished it, and equipped it with laundry appliances so that she could go back into business without applying for welfare support.

The Red Cross, incidentally, spent $1,682,000 on relief work in New England and Long Island after the 1938 hurricane, and almost one million dollars was collected in contributions to a special hurricane fund from people all over the world. Among the gifts was a twenty-five-dollar check from a Japanese merchant in Honolulu "for people who have got trouble in New England."

Many owners of shorefront property suffered considerable losses in real estate that disappeared during the hurricane. The coast lines of Long Island and New England were so changed by the storm that new maps had to be drawn hurriedly in the following months. Great Gull Island, the Army's coast artillery post between the north fork of Long Island and Fishers Island, was reduced in size from 18 acres to 12 acres. Three sisters in Connecticut who owned a shorefront tract of 50 acres, which they had been planning to put up for sale, found themselves after the hurricane with 2 acres. Frederick W. Gay, of Pawtuxet, Rhode Island, had agreed to buy two waterfront lots in front of his summer home at Bay Ridge two weeks before the storm, and on Tuesday, September 20, he paid for the land and received the deed. The lots formed a strip of beach 165 feet long and 50 feet deep, with a sand bluff 12 feet above the beach on one end, and at the other end, a dune rising 20 feet. The next day the hurricane took away all the new property that Gay had just bought, including the two high dunes, and left his original lot flattened and on the beach at water level.

But for several months after the storm prosperity was

enjoyed by building contractors, carpenters, masons, and roofers who were summoned to repair damaged houses. In many towns lumber, shingles, and nails, along with lanterns and flashlights, were hard to find. A factory in Walpole, Massachusetts, which produced roofing materials, was shipping out shingles at the rate of 1,200 to 2,200 tons a day for several days after the hurricane, an all-time record. (A man in Woburn, Massachusetts, looking out a window at the hurricane, remarked to his wife that an unusually large number of pigeons were flying around the neighborhood. Then he exclaimed, "Those aren't pigeons! They're shingles!") Hardware stores were besieged for axes and saws, which were needed for the removal of uprooted trees. A Boston newspaper reported the saga of a resident of Marlboro —a town near Worcester on Route 20, the old Boston Post Road —who left his home on the day after the hurricane, explaining that he was going downtown to buy an axe and would be back in a few minutes. Having found no axes in Marlboro, he drove east on the Post Road, stopping at hardware stores in Wayland, Weston, and Waltham. All were out of axes. Aroused and determined, the man pressed on to Watertown and from there to Cambridge, where he grimly headed across the Charles River into Boston. After trying several stores in Boston, he finally found one, thirty miles from his home, that had an axe for sale and he bought it.

New England's biggest and sorest loss in the hurricane, next to its loss in lives, was its fallen trees. The United States Forest Service estimated that there was enough timber knocked down by the storm to build 200,000 five-room houses. New Hampshire lost half of its white pines. The city of Springfield, Massachusetts, had 16,000 fallen shade trees. Many of the destroyed trees were famous ones, such as the Sentinel Pine at the Flume in Franconia Notch, New Hampshire, and the Avery Oak in Dedham, Massachusetts, which had been spared in 1796 from being used as timber for the Navy's frigate *Constitution*. New England's apple crop was almost a total loss. In Boston sought-after hurricane souvenirs, which sold for as much as five dollars each, were the metal horticultural name plates taken off trees uprooted from the Boston Common and the Public Gardens. The roots of a fallen tree on Lake View Avenue in Cambridge exposed a previously covered and long-forgotten grave with a stone that was marked 1833 and bore the names of a couple named Elvira and Warren Robey. In one New England city a lady telephoned a lumber company and asked how much it would pay her for two large fallen trees on her front lawn. Actually, most of the timber felled by the hurricane was too splintered to be used, except as firewood or as pulp at a paper mill.

On Long Island the handsome village of East Hampton mourned the sixty-eight tall and stately elms that had been felled along its main street. A storm had given and a storm had taken away: many of the elms had come from England as saplings in the cargo of a ship wrecked on the East Hampton ocean beach more than one hundred years earlier. East Hampton, the most sedate and exclusive of the summer colonies in the Hamptons, looked down its nose at the allegedly more gaudy Southampton and scarcely acknowledged the existence of Westhampton. After the hurricane Dorothy Quick, a local poetess, overheard two East Hampton ladies lamenting the storm damage in the town. One of them said, "We've so much to be thankful for—East Hampton had practically no loss of life while Westhampton had so much of it."

"Oh, I don't know," the other woman replied crisply.

"Human beings reproduce quickly, but it takes a hundred years to make trees like we had."

Farther west on Long Island, at Patchogue, a young woman became enraged when the early gales of the hurricane threatened to blow down a newly planted tree on her front lawn. Quickly donning rubber boots, a raincoat, and an oilskin hat, she rushed outdoors and stood beside the tree for the rest of the storm, firmly grasping the slim trunk and holding it upright.

One business that gained a lasting benefit from the hurricane of 1938 was air travel. During the period after the storm when railroad service between New York and Boston was interrupted, thousands of people were forced to travel to and from New England by plane for the first time in their lives. After having been pushed into flying and having found it not as uncomfortable as they had suspected, many of them continued to travel by air instead of by rail in the years that followed.

Before the hurricane, air travel in the United States was still in its adolescence. American Airlines, which then held an exclusive franchise on the route between New York and Boston, usually carried about two hundred passengers a day on its flights in both directions between those cities. On the day after the hurricane more than one thousand passengers flew from New York to Boston, and several hundred more flew from Boston to New York. During the following week, the busiest ever experienced by a commercial airline in the United States up to that time, American Airlines was swamped with such a great demand for reservations to and from Boston that it had to waive its exclusive right to the route and call on Trans World, Eastern, and United airlines for help in carrying the load. It was estimated that at least 60 per cent of the new influx of passengers had never been inside a plane before.

*　　*　　*　　*

After the hurricane a humorous panhandler paraded on Boston Common wearing a sign that said, "For 25 cents, I will listen to your story of the hurricane." Everybody who had been in the hurricane had a story to tell and told it repeatedly for years afterward. ("The lights went out," the dentist said, "and there I was holding a flashlight in one hand and trying to pull this fellow's tooth with my other hand, when all of a sudden the window blew in and. . . .") Many of the familiar stories described incidents on Long Island or in Connecticut that were curiously similar to happenings reported in Rhode Island or Massachusetts. One such anecdote, told in many places, concerns the fisherman who came to the temporary morgue at the high-school auditorium and solemnly viewed a body that had been identified as his. "Nope," he said. " 'Taint me." There are countless stories about odd sights in the debris left by the storm, such as the bathroom that was carried from a beach cottage to the middle of the main street in Westhampton, arriving intact with toothbrushes hanging on their rack over the washbasin, the cake of soap in its dish, the curtains still hanging at the window, and the bath mat undisturbed on the floor beside the tub. At the summer resort of Cherry Grove on Fire Island—where a bartender in the hotel slept safely and soundly through the deluge of the hurricane surf—a lamp was found balanced on one edge of its base on a slanted shelf in a tilted cottage. After staring in disbelief at the suspended balance of the lamp, the owner of the cottage picked it up and made several attempts to replace it in

141

the same position, but found that balancing the lamp on its side as it had been left by the waves and the wind was impossible.

A man at Mastic, Long Island, saw both of his artificial legs carried out of his cottage by the tide. Four days later they were found, lying side by side, on a beach at East Moriches, ten miles away.

There were many stories of people from New England who hurried home from Florida to escape the hurricane when it was threatening Miami on Monday, only to find it blowing down their houses on Wednesday. A Long Island woman stopped her car at a public garage in Bridgehampton when the hurricane was getting serious and asked for shelter. When the doors of the garage were opened for her, the rear wall blew out and the front windows collapsed and shattered. The embarrassed woman backed her car away, saying, "I guess I've done enough damage," and drove on down the road. Another woman was left alone in a beach house at Westhampton during the hurricane because her husband was at work in New York City. Frightened by the storm waves dashing across the dunes around the house, she wrote a farewell letter to her husband and nailed it to a rafter. The house survived the storm and so did she. The next morning a rescue party arrived to take her back to the mainland in a boat. Leaving the house, she paused thoughtfully for a moment and then went back inside and carefully tore up the letter.

At the time of the hurricane, the rector of the Cathedral of Saints Peter and Paul in Providence, the Reverend Thomas F. McKitchen, was vacationing with his mother at a cottage on Conimicut Point on Narragansett Bay. They escaped from the surge of storm waves in a rowboat, carrying with them their pet canary, and made their way across the bay to West Barrington. There the priest and his mother and the canary were given shelter in the home of a family named Gilman. After the Mc-Kitchens and the Gilmans retired for the night, thankful that all of them had survived the storm, the Gilmans' cat ate the McKitchens' canary.

One of the stories from Westhampton Beach, printed in *The New York Times* after the hurricane, reminded readers of Sir James Barrie's play *The Admirable Crichton*; the *Times* story described a butler, Arni Benedictson, who took capable command of the situation when a group of more than twenty wealthy socialites and their servants took refuge in his employer's beach house. The butler calmed them and led the party across a collapsing bridge to the mainland a few minutes before the house was washed away. Among the people saved by Benedictson was the Countess Charles de Ferry de Fontnouvelle, wife of the French consul in New York, who had fled from her own cottage earlier in the storm, carrying her twenty-three-month-old daughter. The countess praised the butler's cool leadership and bravery, hailing him as the "hero of everything." The next day, like the admirable Crichton, the butler was quietly back at work at his employer's Park Avenue winter home, acting as if nothing particularly unusual had happened.

Among the other heroes of the storm were a colony of beavers at Palisades Interstate Park near Stony Point on the Hudson River. Apparently the beavers had known about the approach of the hurricane when nobody else had been aware of it. On the night before the storm, park officials found later, the animal engineers worked hard reinforcing several dams that they had already built to control the flow of streams that drained into the Hudson and Ramapo rivers. Their hasty emergency work before the hurricane's downpour prevented floods that might have washed out at least one bridge and three highways.

Another animal hero was a small terrier who was with his owner, Mrs. Peter Kelly, on a schooner in the harbor of Port Washington, Long Island, when the storm struck. Mrs. Kelly found it impossible to hold the boat offshore with three anchors. She tied a rope around the terrier's neck and the dog swam ashore with it, enabling a group of men on a dock to pull the boat in safely.

One of the more gruesome stories of the hurricane described the experience of a survivor at a demolished beach resort. He was thrown into the water and swam to a large wooden plank that he saw floating near him. Having climbed up on it gratefully, he found the board crawling with red ants. The insects swarmed over him, and he had to dive back into the water to escape them.

A dairy farmer from Newport, who was driving his prize-winning bull back to Rhode Island from the Brockton Fair in Massachusetts, encountered the towering surge of waves on Narragansett Bay while crossing a bridge at Tiverton. The farmer found himself swimming in the bay and tried to reach his truck, which was drifting some distance away from him, to release the bellowing bull. Just then another huge wave appeared, carrying a big empty yacht on top of its crest. The yacht crashed down upon the truck, and neither the truck nor the bull was ever seen again.

On the dunes at East Hampton, the swimming pool of the Maidstone Club was filled with bluefish and striped bass after the storm. The owner of a nearby shorefront house found several large fish swimming in his dining room; a snake, dry and comfortable, was curled up on the dining room table. After the hurricane the refugees at the hospital of the Society for the Prevention of Cruelty to Animals at Springfield, Massachusetts, included seventy-one dogs, six turkeys, forty-five cats, two guinea pigs, thirty-one hens, and one horse. The horse had been there once before, during the 1936 flood of the Connecticut River.

At Amherst College it was reported that a group of incoming freshmen taking an intelligence test at the height of the hurricane scored a higher average mark than any freshmen in the previous history of the college, and five points higher than another group of freshmen who took a similar test three days later. The hurricane had no discouraging effect on the competitors engaged that day in an international egg-laying contest at Connecticut State College. All through the storm the champion hens continued to lay eggs at their usual spectacular rate.

On Fire Island a man claimed that he had managed to build a summer cottage—at a total cost of sixty-five cents—from lumber and other building materials that he had salvaged from wreckage on the beach after the hurricane. The sixty-five cents was spent on putty for the windows. Two cottages at New Silver Beach on Buzzards Bay, battered and dislodged from their foundations but still intact, were sold after the storm for twenty-five cents. The sale price did not include the two lots, of course.

The hurricane brought a startling revelation to the circulation managers of the Boston *Post*, which then described itself as New England's great breakfast table newspaper. Every morning since the turn of the century, the *Post* had been sending by train bundles of newspapers addressed to various rural storekeepers in Maine, New Hampshire, and Vermont. When the railroads were disrupted by the hurricane, the newspapers were delivered over the road by trucks, and the management assigned employees to ride with each driver to see that the newspapers were left at the door of each customer in the country villages. The trucking expeditions learned that the *Post* had been sending shipments of newspapers every day to news dealers who had been dead or out of business for as long as twenty-five years.

On the night after the hurricane a group of burglars, like robbers in a Peter Sellers film comedy, tried to crack a safe in a bank at Hillburn, New York, with an electrically powered detonator. Not until they had broken into the bank and made all the preliminary preparations did one of the thieves discover that the detonator was useless because there was no electricity in the wall sockets. For several days after the storm, brides marched down the aisle without music because there was no electric power in the church organs. Since electric refrigerators were useless, ice companies did a big business. All over the hurricane-swept area, people forgot to turn off the switches on lights and electrical appliances when the electricity went off during the storm on Wednesday afternoon. In homes where the power came on again a week or ten days later at two or three o'clock in the morning, families awakened in a blaze of lights shining all over the house, with electric mixers and washing machines whirring and the blare of dance music on the radio in the living room.

After the hurricane Long Island faced a perplexing problem: How could the many holes in the barrier beach between Fire Island Inlet and the new inlet at Shinnecock Bay off the Hamptons be plugged? With so many wide break-throughs running from the ocean to the bays behind the long stretch of beach, there was danger that the storm-leveled dunes would be washed away entirely if hit by another hurricane.

Robert Moses, New York's controversial public works builder, unveiled a grand scheme for saving the beach. He proposed dredging a navigation channel in the bays behind the dunes all the way from Fire Island Inlet to Shinnecock Bay; the

146

dredged sand would be used to fill in the newly broken inlets and to raise the dunes to a height of fourteen feet. Moses also suggested building a concrete highway on top of the dunes to protect them from another hurricane. Moses's proposal was turned down by the Suffolk County supervisors as too expensive and too grandiose.

Cost-cutting conservatives argued that the broken inlets along the fifty miles of beach could be filled with stumps and brush, topped with dredged sand from the bays. This was the tried and true old-fashioned way of building up dunes on beaches, so why wouldn't it work under water too?

It didn't work at all; brush and stumps were too buoyant under the water of the inlets and were easily swept away by the swift current before they could be covered with dredged sand. A new idea was tried, and it finally worked successfully. Sandbags weighted down between layers of old abandoned automobiles from junk yards were dropped into the break-throughs as a foundation for the dredged sand. Even the old cars, with their heavy engines in them, were immediately carried away by the tidal flow when they were first dropped into the inlets by cranes, but gradually, as more automobiles were piled up around the bags of sand, the gaps left by the hurricane began to be plugged and filled. By the spring of 1939 the barrier beach off Long Island was healed.

*   *   *   *

On most tables of hurricane statistics, the deaths and destruction of the hurricane of 1938 are listed in conveniently round figures. The dead are counted at 600, including about

100 missing persons whose bodies were never found, and damages are estimated at about $300,000,000. Actually both estimates should be considerably higher. An authoritative source, a scientific study of east-coast tropical cyclonic storms by two outstanding Weather Bureau meteorologists—*Atlantic Hurricanes*, by Gordon E. Dunn and Banner I. Miller—estimates the 1938 hurricane's toll of dead and missing persons in the New England states at 585—380 in Rhode Island, 99 in Massachusetts, 85 in Connecticut, 14 in New Hampshire, 7 in Vermont, and none in Maine. At least another 50 were counted as dead or missing after the storm in eastern Long Island, and there were many others killed at sea and on the gale-swept shores of New Jersey and New York, including 10 victims in the New York City area and the 18 scallop fishermen from Brooklyn who were drowned off Nantucket during the hurricane. If an exact count of deaths resulting from the storm could be made, the total would probably be closer to 700 than to 600. Another 1,754 people were injured, and an estimated 63,000 people, many of them left homeless, were forced to seek emergency help and shelter from the Red Cross and various local relief agencies.

Estimates of the cost of the 1938 hurricane in property damage have been as high as $382,000,000, and it must be remembered that those estimates were made at the depressed prices of 1938, when the cost of repairing damage was far lower than it is today. The similar hurricane named Carol, which struck Long Island and New England on August 31, 1954, was responsible for far less widespread destruction than the hurricane of 1938, but its damage cost was $450,000,000. The generally accepted figure for the damage done by the hurricane of 1938 is about one third of a billion dollars. The Red Cross estimates that 4,500 homes, summer cottages, and farm buildings were completely destroyed by the hurricane; 15,139 homes, cottages, and farm buildings were damaged, and 2,605 boats were lost and 3,369 boats damaged.

"Until 1954, the 1938 New England hurricane held the all-time record for storm property damage in the United States, and probably the world as well," Dunn and Miller wrote in *Atlantic Hurricanes.* "If current dollar value were used, the damage was exceeded only by that of Diane—the billion-dollar hurricane of 1955." However, as Dunn and Miller point out elsewhere, Diane was not much of a hurricane compared to the hurricane of 1938 because it did little wind or tidal damage. Diane's heavy damage resulted from its heavy rainfall, which came on the heels of heavy rain from another hurricane, Connie, a few days earlier. The steady downpour started devastating flash floods in the Northeast, particularly in New England, where the floods caused 60 per cent of Diane's billion-dollar damage. But for widespread and costly hurricane damage—the terrifying wreckage by gales and towering surges of storm waves as well as floods—the hurricane of 1938 was by far the most destructive storm of modern times because it swept over such a thickly populated and widespread area. The United States has experienced more powerful hurricanes, such as the one on September 2, 1935, in the Florida Keys and the hurricane named Camille, which demolished the Gulf Coast of Mississippi on August 17, 1969, probably the most intense tropical cyclonic disturbances ever recorded in the Western Hemisphere. But none of the other big ones killed and terrorized so many people in so many crowded states as the 1938 tropical storm did in the Northeast.

The great loss of lives was caused not only by the unexpectedness of the disaster; people also failed to take precautions because they had no idea that the storm might be, or could be, a hurricane. There was a sharp decline in the number of fatalities when other big tropical storms struck the northeast coast in later years mainly because people had learned in 1938 that their area was not immune from the kind of hurricane that they had associated, until then, only with Florida and the Gulf Coast. Carol in 1954, which hit the same places on Long Island and in New England, left sixty instead of more than six hundred dead. Many people who survived the hurricane in 1938 said that they had had their biggest fright after the storm when they learned that it had been a hurricane. "I was having the grandest time walking around town during the storm," a woman in East Providence said to a local reporter. "When I got home and found out what had been happening all over, and realized it was a hurricane, I fainted. If I knew it was a hurricane, I wouldn't have gone out in it for a million dollars."

Survivors of the worst experiences in the 1938 hurricane feel that it paid them a compensation. Joan Schmid Coleman, who was on the beach at Westhampton during the storm, said recently, "I feel so lucky to be alive that since the hurricane nothing in this life has ever really bothered me." Mrs. Geoffrey Moore, writing to her brother about her escape from the disaster at Napatree Point, ended her letter with these words: "I sometimes feel that we have had a preview of the end of the world. We certainly saw how easily it could happen, and in such a short time. We shall never forget the feeling of helplessness in the face of the elements let loose. We who have been through this hurricane, I am sure, have gained a deeper, richer, more complete outlook on life than we ever could have gained otherwise."

5

*T*HE EMBARRASSED United States Weather Bureau was hit by
a barrage of public criticism after the hurricane of 1938 for its
failure to provide a warning before the storm struck Long Island
and New England. "In the long and laudable annals of the government's weather forecasters that day's record makes what must
be the sorriest page," John Q. Stewart, then a professor of astro-
nomical physics at Princeton University, wrote in *Harper's
Magazine.* "Seven states, and the Province of Quebec, counted
close to seven hundred fatalities. A seaboard as wealthy as any
in the world, and its hinterland, heavily provided with telephones, radios, coastguards and State police, felt the shock.
There had been no warning worth the mentioning; telephones
and coastguards were scarcely called to service. A sophisticated
population died by the hundreds with little or no knowledge of
what raw shape of death this was which struck from the sky and
the tide."

Stewart speculated on what the federal government's reaction might have been if the New York Stock Exchange, instead of the Department of Agriculture's Weather Bureau, had been responsible for broadcasting storm warnings. "The outcry from Washington over the insufficiency of the warning would have been immediate, bitter and voluminous," the Princeton physicist wrote. "Scores of previous lifesaving predictions of hurricanes along the sparsely populated Southern coasts would have been dismissed as insignificant."

In replying to its many critics, the Weather Bureau blamed the lack of advance warning on the sudden and unpredictable burst of speed with which the hurricane had rushed north after leaving Cape Hatteras on the morning of September 21. Later calculations showed that after the Weather Bureau had lost track of the storm off the Carolina coast, it had covered the 425 miles from there to Long Island in less than seven hours—an average speed of 61 miles per hour. "Had the storm not moved with such unprecedented rapidity," the acting chief of the Weather Bureau in Washington, C. C. Clark, wrote in a letter a few weeks after the hurricane, "there can be no doubt that Weather Bureau warnings by radio and through the press would have reached nearly everyone in the affected area."

The critics felt, however, that the Weather Bureau's failure in 1938 was due mainly to its general attitude of indifference toward the danger of a hurricane reaching the northeast coast. Newspapers in New England complained that there had been no lack of warning when the same hurricane had threatened Florida a few days earlier, but after the storm left the southern coast and headed north, the Weather Bureau had seemed to lose interest in it. The editors of the Hartford *Courant* became incensed over a report that the Hartford office of the Weather Bureau had not issued a warning of the hurricane for fear of causing a local panic. "It appears that the United States Weather Bureau frowns on predictions of disasters in these parts although it encourages them in Florida," the *Courant* remarked tartly. Actually the Hartford office of the Weather Bureau had no authority to issue a hurricane warning; local Weather Bureau chiefs in the Northeast could only call attention to hurricane warnings issued from the bureau's main office in Washington, which was responsible for coastal weather forecasts north of Cape Hatteras. As John Daily, the Weather Bureau chief at Providence, said at the time, he had issued no hurricane warnings in Rhode Island because he had received none from Washington. "With the available information that was on hand," Daily said, "no one thought that the storm would be so severe."

One of the sharpest and most carefully documented criticisms of the Weather Bureau's handling of reports on the storm appeared in the appendix to *The Hurricane of 1938 on Eastern Long Island,* a book by Ernest S. Clowes, who was then the publisher of the weekly *Hampton Press* at Bridgehampton. Clowes was also associated with the Weather Bureau as one of its cooperative observers on Long Island and was an experienced student of meteorology. He compiled a detailed review of Weather Bureau reports on the hurricane from the time of the first warning of its approach to the Florida coast on Saturday, September 17, until the storm reached Long Island on the following Wednesday afternoon.

In his critical review Clowes pointed out that in 1938 the Weather Bureau's forecasts and warnings of tropical storms were issued from its Florida station at Jacksonville when such storms were off the coast south of Cape Hatteras. When a hurricane moved north of Cape Hatteras, it became the responsibility of the bureau's main forecasting center in Washington. Clowes noted emphatically that there was a marked contrast between the urgently vigilant warnings about the hurricane of 1938 issued in Jacksonville and the mild forecasts on the probable course and character of the same storm that were put out later in Washington. When compared to the forcefulness and definiteness of the Jacksonville reports, Clowes said, "Washington's attitude seems a bit casual."

The forecasters at the Jacksonville office had issued frequent and strongly precautionary reports on the hurricane, not only when it was heading toward Miami on September 18 and 19, but after it turned northward on Monday night. All day Tuesday, as the storm moved toward the Georgia and Carolina coasts, the Florida weather observers continued to put out warnings of its dangerous intensity. On Tuesday night the Jacksonville office predicted that the center of the hurricane would pass near "but east" of Cape Hatteras on Wednesday, and added that it would apparently "gradually turn northeastward and move rapidly in the next twenty-four hours." In their last advisory report on the hurricane, issued at 3 A.M.* on September 21 before the tracking of the storm was turned over to the Washington office of the bureau, the forecasters in Jacksonville indicated that they were no longer so certain that the center of the storm would curve off to the east and pass safely out to sea. They reported that the hurricane was then 275 miles south of Cape Hatteras and "moving rapidly north," and only possibly "east of north." This last word from Jacksonville on the hurricane predicted accurately that the center would pass near but slightly off the Carolina capes within the next twelve hours, attended by dangerous gales and high tides on the coast and "by hurricane

* Times given in reference to Weather Bureau reports are Eastern Standard Time.

winds short distance offshore." The Florida station signed off advising caution to ships "in path of this severe storm."

Then the Washington office took over from Jacksonville, and as Clowes noted in his review, the word "hurricane" disappeared from further reports on the storm. An advisory report at 9 A.M. on September 21 referred to the disturbance on the coast as a "tropical storm" rather than as a hurricane, which was what Jacksonville had been calling it until six hours earlier. Washington did mention, however, that the "tropical storm" had "winds of hurricane force" near its center.

Later in the morning, at eleven thirty, another advisory report from Washington dropped the mention of hurricane winds. This report placed the center of the storm about one hundred miles east of the Virginia capes and said that it was "moving rapidly northward or slightly east of north" attended by winds "of whole gale force." Whole gales are less than the hurricane minimum force of seventy-five miles per hour. The last report on the storm issued by the Weather Bureau in Washington—at 2 P.M., when the hurricane gales were already blowing people and houses off the beaches on Long Island—said erroneously that the "tropical storm" was east-southeast of Atlantic City and "moving rapidly north-northeast with no material change in intensity since morning." It added that the storm would "likely pass over Long Island and Connecticut late [that] afternoon or early [that night] attended by shifting gales." That prediction was one of the great understatements of recent times.

As all meteorologists agreed later, the thing that drew the hurricane so rapidly on a course straight north to Long Island and New England was the inviting carpet of moist and warm low-pressure atmosphere stretching that day from New England to Cape Hatteras; the block that kept the storm from turning off to the east, as the Weather Bureau had assumed it would, was a plateau of dry high-pressure air over the North Atlantic south of Nova Scotia. In its own general review of weather conditions on the east coast issued Tuesday night, before the hurricane raced north from Cape Hatteras, the Weather Bureau itself described these low-pressure and high-pressure areas. The Washington forecasters even pointed out in their general survey on that night before September 21 that the low pressure reached down to the edge of the hurricane. "A broad trough of low pressure extends from New England south-southwestward to the tropical disturbance," the Washington report said. "Pressure remains high . . . from Nova Scotia and Newfoundland and southward and southeastward over the ocean." But apparently it never occurred to anybody in the Weather Bureau office in Washington that these low and high areas might draw the tropical disturbance into New England.

"The contrast between the handling of the hurricane from Jacksonville and from Washington is apparent," Ernest Clowes wrote in concluding his critique of the Weather Bureau, "but in fairness it should be said that the Washington office was rather in the dark Wednesday morning as to the movements of the storm. . . . The two ship reports (that it did receive on the hurricane's position that morning) were somewhat misleading. Both indicated that the storm was losing rather than gaining intensity. Whatever the reasons, the almost consistent underestimate of the storm's intensity and speed of travel by the Washington office is in marked contrast with the attitude of the Jacksonville forecaster. In all the warnings from Washington the word 'hurricane' is used but once (and then to describe winds rather than the character of the storm itself). It is also notable that until the wind was blowing at hurricane force over Long Island, neither that long coast line nor that of Connecticut was specifically mentioned in any warning."

As Clowes suggested, the Washington office of the Weather Bureau did not take the northbound hurricane too seriously because there had been no reports from ships at sea indicating that the storm was not turning away from the coast at Cape Hatteras as tropical disturbances from Florida usually do. Over the previous century so few severe hurricanes on the Atlantic coast had failed to make that safe east turn away from the Carolina capes that the Weather Bureau had come to assume that every tropical storm would do so, unless there was very strong and definite evidence to the contrary. Thus in 1938 a hurricane off Cape Hatteras was regarded as nothing to get excited about— it was bound to blow out to sea sooner or later.

The savage surprise attack of the hurricane of 1938 on Long Island and New England did not immediately bring about any sweeping reforms in the Weather Bureau's methods of tracking and forecasting hurricanes. For the next few years the bureau had to go on predicting the probable behavior of such storms merely on the basis of voluntary reports from ships at sea, which were often scarce or unreliable. Better technical methods of obtaining data on tropical storms had to await the tracking of potentially dangerous low-pressure disturbances by aircraft surveillance and by radar, which did not come into systematic use by the Weather Bureau until after World War II. The unexpected storm disaster of 1938 did, however, perform one invaluable service that was to change the concepts of hurricane forecasting on the Atlantic coast and save countless lives in later years. It destroyed for all time the dangerous assumption, accepted so complacently before then, that big tropical cyclonic storms were not likely to threaten the heavily populated shores north of Cape Hatteras.

The lesson taught in 1938 was learned none too soon. Over the next thirty years there were many more destructive hurricanes from Florida and the Caribbean that failed to make the right turn at the Carolina capes. On September 8, 1944, a bigger and much wider hurricane than the one in 1938 swept up the coast from the Carolinas, heading toward the bulge of New England's south shores. Wartime security restrictions prevented the broadcasting of weather reports to the public, so it was impossible to spread an adequate alarm. Luckily the center of the 1944 hurricane veered far enough to the northeast—only glancing off the coasts of New York and New England—to do relatively little damage ashore compared to the destruction in 1938. But it killed 390 people in New England and 63 others in nearby Atlantic coast states. The 1944 hurricane was one of the first of such storms to be closely observed in action by Air Force weather reconnaissance planes. An Air Force plane that flew into the storm's inner circle of 140-mile-per-hour winds was almost torn apart. When the plane returned to its base, it was found to have had 150 rivets ripped from one wing.

The development of systematic aircraft reconnaissance and radar tracking during the postwar years greatly increased the efficiency of the Weather Bureau's expanded hurricane-watching facilities. By the 1950's, when the Atlantic and Gulf coasts were devastated by a series of severe tropical cyclones, the Weather Bureau had established its custom, annoying to many women, of identifying hurricanes by feminine names. The worst seasons of northbound hurricanes in that storm-wracked decade were in 1954, the year of Carol, Edna, and Hazel, and in 1955, when floods caused by the combined rainfalls of Connie and Diane did a billion dollars worth of damage in the Northeast.

Today's meteorologists, in defending the Weather Bureau of 1938, argue that the 1938 storm's sudden and unpredictable burst of forward speed in its final dash from Cape Hatteras to Long Island would have baffled any forecasters, no matter how vigilant they might have been. The similar behavior of Carol in 1954 under much more careful and constant scrutiny was held up to illustrate the hazards of hurricane forecasting in a discussion by Robert H. Simpson at a UNESCO meeting in Tokyo later that year. Simpson, an authority on hurricanes, is now the Weather Bureau's director of the National Hurricane Warning Center at Coral Gables, near Miami. He was talking to the UNESCO group about the economic problems involved in putting a thickly populated and industrialized coastal area on a hurricane emergency alert that could turn out to be unnecessary if the hurricane wavered only slightly from its predicted path, as hurricanes usually do.

"For example, the City of Miami requires a full twelve to eighteen hours notice to prepare adequately for a hurricane, and does so at a cost of three quarters of a million dollars," Simpson said. "A difference of only a few degrees in a storm heading over a twenty-four-hour period can mean that these expensive precautions will be made uselessly. Or consider the case of the Dow Chemical Company on the highly industrialized Texas coast. This company's large plastics plant is vulnerable to high water from hurricanes. As little as ten miles variation in the track of a storm can spell the difference between this plant having to close down or remain open. To close the plant costs the company more than $900,000. Finally, consider the case of Hurricane Carol, which in late August of this year formed in the Bahama Islands. This storm moved stealthily and with indecision slowly north-

ward off the capes of North Carolina before surging suddenly
ahead and roaring across the Long Island and New England
coasts with a destructive intensity equalled on only two previous
occasions in [history]—1815 and 1938. The last four hundred
miles of its movement over water was covered in a little more
than twelve hours. The forecast problem in this case was especially critical. If the storm, during the last twelve hours of movement, had followed a heading less than ten degrees to the right
of its actual path, New England would have escaped virtually
unscathed. In fifty years, fifty-four other storms approached the
North Carolina capes along the same general path as Carol, yet
failed to affect New England seriously."

In other words, no matter how vigilantly and scientifi-
cally a hurricane is tracked, it is still hard to pinpoint its
actual course. In many respects, Carol in 1954 was the hurricane of 1938 all over again. It upset the forecasts and arrived
long before it was expected. Once again the elms in East Hampton were knocked down, Montauk was marooned, cottages were
swept off Misquamicut Beach, the casino at Newport was destroyed, and downtown Providence was flooded. The spire on the
Old North Church in Boston was toppled. But there was one big
difference. This time the number of casualties was small—sixty
dead instead of more than six hundred—because the people on
Long Island and in New England were paying attention to the
hurricane when it was lurking off Cape Hatteras and they were
taking precautions before it made its final move.

A few days after Carol's departure, New England was
alerted for a hurricane named Dolly. Beaches on Buzzards Bay
were vacated and the Red Cross established an emergency re-
gional relief headquarters at New Bedford. Dolly never came.
She curved off to the northeast of Nova Scotia. On September 11,

eleven days after Carol's visit, another big and intense hurricane named Edna was moving toward Nantucket after narrowly missing the shores of the Carolinas. Fortunately, Edna stayed to the east of the New England mainland, hitting only the tip of Cape Cod, the Bay of Maine, and Eastport, at Maine's far down-East point.

The Weather Bureau, with the aid of Navy and Air Force weather reconnaissance planes, did a remarkably effective job of spreading advance warnings across the eastern states from the Carolinas to Canada ahead of the eighth and most destructive storm of the 1954 hurricane season. This was the incredibly long-lived hurricane named Hazel, which totally demolished several villages and killed hundreds of people in Haiti before crossing North Carolina, Virginia, Pennsylvania, New York State, and Ontario. The storm center was first spotted in its early formative stages by a Navy Hurricane Hunter plane near Grenada, not far from the coast of Venezuela, on October 5; it was carefully followed and watched by other air reconnaissance observers during the next ten days, as it wandered west over the Caribbean Sea and then turned north, sweeping over Haiti and the Bahamas before hitting the North Carolina coast south of Wilmington, near the Cape Fear area.

The course of the hurricane was so well plotted and under such constant surveillance from aircraft that the coast line on both sides of Cape Fear, from Myrtle Beach, South Carolina, to the Morehead City-Beaufort area of North Carolina, was carefully warned and prepared for the storm many hours before the first gales and high surges of waves began to hit that stretch of shore. The damage on the coast was almost unbelievable. Every fishing dock between Myrtle Beach and Cedar Island, North Carolina, a distance of 170 miles, was destroyed. At Carolina

Beach 475 buildings were destroyed and 1,365 others were damaged; 100,000 cubic yards of beach sand was piled in drifts more than six feet high on the streets and highways. On Long Beach 300 new concrete-block homes with concrete floors and paved driveways were completely swept away, leaving no debris behind. The winds at many places reached heights of 140 and 150 miles per hour. But because the destroyed area on the coasts of North and South Carolina had been so well alerted before the hurricane, there were only 19 lives lost. In fact Hazel, which moved on across Virginia, a few miles west of Washington, and over Pennsylvania and New York to Toronto, was able to kill a total of only 94 people in the United States.

The Weather Bureau began to use radar stations on the ground for tracking hurricanes in 1955, and it now has sixteen integrated radar posts covering the coast from Eastport, Maine, to Brownsville, Texas. This system makes it almost impossible for a hurricane to approach any point on the Atlantic or Gulf of Mexico shore lines without warning. Radar, of course, is also used in hurricane-tracking aircraft and weather ships. The position of a hurricane's eye can be pinpointed on a radarscope 190 miles or more away from the storm. Recent hurricanes have been under continuous radar surveillance while traveling off the coast from Puerto Rico to Nantucket.

The most exciting and the most important event in the whole history of hurricane spotting, however, took place early on the morning of April 10, 1960, when Weather Bureau scientists at Fort Monmouth, New Jersey, discovered that a fully developed hurricane was situated at sea eight hundred miles east of Brisbane, Australia. The hurricane, or typhoon, as hurricanes are called in that part of the Pacific Ocean, had been photographed by Tiros I, the new weather-reporting satellite that was circling the earth. The satellite, equipped with television, had sent the picture of the hurricane to Fort Monmouth long before anybody in Australia knew of the storm's existence, which was later confirmed by the Australian Meteorological Bureau.

Satellites are making it possible to spot hurricanes in vast and empty areas of the ocean where there are no ships or aircraft to report such dangerous storms. The photographs from a satellite, taken four or five hundred miles above the sea, can show an ocean area of two thousand square miles.

These space-age developments in weather exploration technology, along with the growing wealth of weather-study experience, make meteorologists at the government's National Hurricane Warning Center certain that the exact location where a hurricane will hit a coast line—give or take seventy-five miles— can now be predicted twenty-four hours in advance. Such an advance warning was spread before Camille's recent attack on the Gulf Coast. Times have changed since September 21, 1938.

* * * *

As the tracking and forecasting of hurricanes becomes a more exact science, meteorologists at the National Hurricane Warning Center at Coral Gables are wondering how soon the name of their research institution will be changed to "National Hurricane Prevention Center." Preventing or destroying potentially dangerous hurricanes, or even harnessing their huge forces of energy for industrial or domestic use, seems much more possible in these days of great technical achievements than it seemed a few years ago.

The Weather Bureau and the National Hurricane Warning Center receive many letters suggesting that hurricanes could be

163

destroyed by atomic bombs. A nuclear explosion might indeed break up a new and growing hurricane in the early stages of its formation, but such infant cyclonic storms are hard to find. And an atomic bomb could hardly make a dent in a fully developed hurricane, which in making rain over a twenty-four-hour period uses the equivalent of the force of five hundred atomic bombs of the Nagasaki type. In discussing the energy of hurricanes in their book *Atlantic Hurricanes*, Gordon E. Dunn and Banner I. Miller, both experts on the subject, point out that while an atomic blast has lifted 10,000,000 tons of water, a hurricane has poured 2,500,000,000 tons of water on Puerto Rico within a few hours, and that was only a fraction of the cyclonic storm's total rainfall at the time. Dunn and Miller also mention that an ordinary summer thunderstorm has as much energy as thirteen atomic bombs.

There is also the danger that a nuclear explosion in a hurricane would contaminate the surrounding streams of air with radioactive fallout, creating a greater menace to coastal areas than a hurricane.

A safer method of destroying a hurricane, or diverting its course, has already been tested successfully. This is the process called seeding, the saturation of the storm's rotating cyclonic gales and clouds with dry ice or silver iodide. Seeding could dissipate a hurricane by cooling its heat and inducing its energy to be drained away in rain making, or the same saturation method with silver iodide crystals could be used to change the route of the storm center by weakening one section of its doughnut-shaped pattern. In a few hours the hurricane would regain its full normal shape and return to its previous track, but the temporary diversion might steer it away from a heavily populated coastal area.

Seeding of hurricanes is strongly opposed by many public officials, legislators, and private citizens, and also by many meteorologists, who feel that such tampering with nature could cause a sudden, erratic change in a storm that might be disastrous. The opposition dates back to October, 1947, when a hurricane moving in a safe northeastern course off the coast of northern Florida was seeded with a saturation of dry ice to induce rain and thereupon made a sharp left turn into the shore line near Savannah, Georgia, where it killed one man. It was charged that the seeding had caused the storm's sudden and dangerous change in direction, and there has been vigorous disapproval of such experiments ever since, despite a later study of the 1947 hurricane that argued that the storm was already making its sharp westward turn five or seven hours before the seeding took place. The present policy is to seed hurricanes only at a considerable distance from the nearest shore point.

In their book on hurricane behavior, Dunn and Miller discuss the possibility that widespread artificial destruction of hurricanes might cause a troublemaking imbalance in the transfer of warm air from the tropics to the polar regions. "Heat must be transported poleward to prevent gradual cooling of the poles and gradual warming of the equatorial regions," the meteorologists write. "Hurricanes provide one means of maintaining this balance, although they are not the only means nor in fact the most important. Perhaps it is when other means of maintaining the heat balance begin to fail and heat accumulates in the tropics that hurricanes occur. If hurricane control were successful and none were allowed to go through their full life cycle, nature would undoubtedly find some other method of maintaining the heat balance, and who can say that this new method might not even be more disastrous than the hurricane itself?"

Dunn and Miller also speculate on the fascinating possibility that someday man may be able to create a hurricane, or to capture one and make it stand still, in order to make use of its incredible energy, a source of power much greater than nuclear energy. They point out that a captive hurricane could also solve one of the most pressing problems of the modern world—how to remove the salt from ocean water. "A hurricane does just that," Dunn and Miller say. "Literally, billions of tons of water per day are evaporated from the ocean and drawn into the hurricane circulation, to rise and fall out again as salt-free rain. Collected from a captive hurricane and stored, this water could offer an almost unlimited supply of fresh water for drinking, industry, and irrigation purposes."

It sounds fantastic, but so did travel to the moon only a few years ago.

Acknowledgments

We wish to express our thanks to the many survivors of the hurricane of 1938 who recalled their experiences for this account of the storm; to Mrs. Albert K. Trout, Jr., for permission to use the late George Burghard's report on the day of the hurricane at Westhampton Beach; to Mrs. David C. De Jong for permission to quote from her husband's article on the hurricane in Providence in the September, 1939, issue of *Yankee* magazine; and especially to Marcelle Hammond Ham, editor and publisher of *Seaside Topics*, Watch Hill, Rhode Island, for our use of the personal experience stories compiled by her father, the late Charles F. Hammond, in the special hurricane issue of *Seaside Topics*, which was published in November, 1938. The hurricane issue of *Seaside Topics*, a remarkable report on the storm disaster at Napatree Point, has recently been republished in its entirety and is on sale in pamphlet form at the offices of *Seaside Topics* at Watch Hill. We are also indebted for information on hurricanes in general, and on the hurricane of 1938 in particular, to *Atlantic Hurricanes*, by Gordon E. Dunn and Banner I. Miller, published by the Louisiana State University Press in 1960, and to

The Hurricane of 1938 on Eastern Long Island, by Ernest S. Clowes, published by the Hampton Press, Bridgehampton, New York, in 1939, but now unfortunately out of print. Statistics on the damage done by the hurricane, and reports on relief work after the storm, were obtained from the American National Red Cross *Official Report of Relief Operations, New York and New England Hurricane and Floods of 1938*. Among the many other valuable sources of information used in research for this book were reports on the hurricane of 1938 in *The New York Times*, the Hartford *Courant*, the Providence *Journal*, the Boston *Post*, and the Boston *Globe*, and three magazine articles on the storm, one by John T. Winterich in the *New Yorker*, December 17, 1938, and the others by John Q. Stewart in *Harper's Magazine*, January, 1939, and by F. Barrows Colton in the *National Geographic Magazine*, April, 1939.

—J. McC.